CAPITALIZING ON DISASTER

Cultural Politics & the Promise of Democracy
A Series from Paradigm Publishers
Edited by Henry A. Giroux

Empire and Inequality: America and the World Since 9/11,
Paul Street (2004)

The Terror of Neoliberalism,
Henry A. Giroux (2004)

Caught in the Crossfire: Kids, Politics, and America's Future,
Lawrence Grossberg (2005)

*Reading and Writing for Civic Literacy: The Critical Citizen's
Guide to Argumentative Rhetoric,*
Donald Lazere (2005)

*Why Are We Reading Ovid's Handbook on Rape? Teaching and
Learning at a Women's College,*
Madeleine Kahn (2005)

Schooling and the Struggle for Public Life, Updated Edition,
Henry A. Giroux (2005)

*Listening Beyond the Echoes: Media, Ethics, and Agency in an
Uncertain World,*
Nick Couldry (2006)

Michel Foucault: Materialism and Education, Updated Edition,
Mark Olssen (2006)

Pedagogies of the Global: Knowledge in the Human Interest, Arif
Dirlik (2006)

Capitalizing on Disaster: Taking and Breaking Public Schools,
Kenneth J. Saltman (2007)

Patriotic Correctness: Academic Freedom and Its Enemies,
John K. Wilson (2007)

CAPITALIZING ON DISASTER

Taking and Breaking Public Schools

KENNETH J. SALTMAN

Paradigm Publishers
Boulder • London

Copyright © 2007 Paradigm Publishers

Portions of Chapter 2 were originally published in *Review of Education, Pedagogy, and Cultural Studies* 28, no. 1 (2006): 25–56. Reprinted by permission of Taylor and Francis.

Published in the United States by Paradigm Publishers, 3360 Mitchell Lane Suite E, Boulder, CO 80301 USA.

Paradigm Publishers is the trade name of Birkenkamp & Company, LLC, Dean Birkenkamp, President and Publisher.

Library of Congress Cataloging-in-Publication Data
Saltman, Kenneth J., 1969–
    Capitalizing on disaster : taking and breaking public schools / Kenneth J. Saltman.
        p. cm. — (Cultural politics & the promise of democracy)
    Includes bibliographical references and index.
ISBN-13   978-1-59451-381-7 (cloth: alk. paper)
ISBN-10   1-59451-381-3 (cloth: alk. paper)
ISBN-13   978-1-59451-382-4 (pbk.: alk. paper)
ISBN-10   1-59451-382-1 (pbk.: alk. paper)
1. Privatization in education. 2. Disaster relief—Economic aspects.
3. Capitalism. 4. School management and organization. 5. Education—Social aspects. I. Title.
    LB2806.36.S248 2007
    379.73—dc22
                                                                                          2006103209

Printed and bound in the United States of America on acid-free paper that meets the standards of the American National Standard for Permanence of Paper for Printed Library Materials.

Designed and Typeset by Straight Creek Bookmakers.

11 10 09 08 07 1 2 3 4 5

Contents

᪉

Acknowledgments

꘎

I owe a number of people an enormous debt of gratitude for their help with this book. In the winter of 2005, I had the wonderful opportunity to do a Fulbright Research Chair at McMaster University in Hamilton, Ontario. I would like to thank the U.S.-Canada Fulbright Commission for providing me with the time to research and write this book. I am grateful to DePaul University for providing me with a funded research leave to support the project. McMaster University and in particular Imre Szeman, Robert O'Brien, Sara Mayo, and the Institute on Globalization and the Human Condition provided a warm welcome and helpful support. That time in Hamilton also allowed me the immeasurable benefit of being able to be just blocks away from my friends Henry Giroux and Susan Giroux to talk about books and ideas. What a pleasure. Typical of his vast generosity, Henry Giroux gave valuable advice on the manuscript. Thanks to editor Dean Birkenkamp and Beth Davis at Paradigm for their important suggestions for revisions and especially for suggesting the addition of the Chicago chapter. Robin Truth Goodman provided ideas, crucial criticism, close reading, editing, and laughs. She put more time and thought into this project than anyone, so any criticisms, misplaced commas, or logical lapses should certainly be attributed to her alone. My conversations with my former colleague Pauline Lipman about the subject of this book had a very formative impact. Pauline Lipman and Kathy Szybist offered important insights on the relationships between housing and schooling. Highly skilled graduate research assistant Lisa

Short provided valuable research assistance on this project. Nicole Nudo provided crucial administrative and technical support that made this project much easier. Thanks also to my Globalization and Education reading group buddies Max Haiven, Mauricio Martinez, and Laura Bolton. And thanks to the Hamilton Critical Media Studies cohort of Tim Kaposy and Theresa Enright. Thanks also to Enora Brown, Stephen Haymes, Ron Scapp, David Gabbard, Trevor Norris, Deron Boyles, David Hursh, Wayne Ross, Kristen Buras, Chris Murray, Kevin Bunka, and Noah Gelfand.

INTRODUCTION
Smash and Grab

Schooling in Disaster Capitalism

ǝ

Around the world, disaster is providing the means for business to accumulate profit. From the Asian tsunami of 2005 that allowed corporations to seize coveted shoreline properties for resort development to the multibillion-dollar no-bid reconstruction contracts in Iraq and Afghanistan, from the privatization of public schooling following Hurricane Katrina in the Gulf Coast to the ways that No Child Left Behind sets up public schools to be dismantled and made into investment opportunities, a grotesque pattern is emerging in which business is capitalizing on disaster. Naomi Klein has written of the rise of a predatory form of disaster capitalism that uses "the desperation and fear created by catastrophe to engage in radical social and economic engineering. And on this front, the reconstruction industry works so quickly and efficiently that the privatizations and land grabs are usually locked in before the local population knows what hit them."[1]

Although overt attempts to privatize and commercialize public schools continue at an alarming rate, the privatization of public education has increasingly taken a new form that coheres with what Klein terms "disaster capitalism" and what David Harvey describes as "accumulation by dispossession." From the Gulf Coast of the United States to for-profit U.S. educational profiteering in Iraq, from Chicago's Renaissance 2010 plan to the federal No Child Left Behind act, as this book details, the new predatory form of educational

1

privatization aims to dismantle public schools to privatize and commodify them. This book identifies a growing social trend and a right-wing movement.

Part of this right-wing movement of capitalizing on disaster in education involves think tanks. As the following chapters detail, right-wing think tanks such as the Heritage Foundation and the Urban Institute were ready to use Hurricane Katrina to push long-standing public school privatization schemes. Other think tanks, such as the Hoover Institution, the American Enterprise Institute, and the Heartland Institute, rally and plan for business to take advantage of the historical production of disastrous public school conditions in communities subject to long-standing public and private disinvestment. Right-wing politicians spearhead this privatization agenda through the federal No Child Left Behind act.

As part of this movement, some right-wing politicians were able to take advantage of the disaster in the Gulf Coast to seize coveted land and public resources and transfer political power over education to the rich and privileged. Others were able to shunt educational rebuilding opportunities to their former colleagues.

Another dimension of this movement of capitalizing on disaster involves the expanding role of for-profit corporations in enacting right-wing foreign policy and exporting right-wing domestic educational policy overseas. As the second chapter illustrates, a U.S. company, Creative Associates International, Incorporated, made millions on no-bid contracts while engaged in "educational rebuilding" that includes fostering the educational privatization agenda. The human-made disaster of the Iraq war has been a vast moneymaking opportunity not only for companies such as Halliburton and Bechtel but also for educational profiteers.

This movement takes guidance not only from think tanks but from business groups as well. As the third chapter details, the Commercial Club of Chicago and the Metropolitan Planning Council have planned and coordinated the dismantling of predominantly poor, working-class, and nonwhite public schools in Chicago in coordination with the dismantling of public housing. These efforts involve vast privatization and decimation of crucial public services while promising enormous profits for the rich as public resources are funneled to education profiteers, real estate developers, and lawyers.

However, this right-wing movement of capitalizing on disaster should not be exclusively understood as a coordinated effort of rich rightists and ideologues (though in part this conclusion is unavoidable when faced with the evidence presented here). This movement also needs to be understood in relation to the broader political, ideological, and cultural formations most prevalent at the moment—namely, neoliberalism and neoconservatism. As I contend in each chapter, this right-wing movement imperils the development of public schools as crucial sites for engaged critical democracy while undermining the public purposes of public education and amassing vast profits for few, and even furthering U.S. foreign policy agendas.

Progressive and liberal educators concerned with defending and expanding public education as a necessary element of a democratic society may be relieved over a number of relatively recent political and economic failures of the educational privatization movement. At the turn of the millennium, the business press was describing public education as the next big haul, ripe for privatization and commodification, comparing it to the health care and defense sectors and suggesting that it promised $600 billion a year in possible takings.[2] Yet, it is clear just a few years later that the educational management organization (EMO), aiming to run public schools for profit, is not overtaking public education (though it is growing at an alarming rate of a fivefold increase in schools managed in six years). The largest experiment in running schools for profit, The Edison Schools, continues on as a hobbled symbol, according to the business press, of why running schools for profit on a wide scale is not particularly profitable.[3] The massive EMO Knowledge Universe, created by junk bond felon Michael Milken, is in the midst of going out of business.[4] The voucher movement, which the Right has been pushing for decades, had only, until the autumn of 2005, been able to capture the Washington, D.C., public schools with the largesse of Congress—and that experiment is by all accounts looking bad. Even school commercialism is taking a hit from a public fed up with shameless attempts of marketers to sell sugar-laden soft drinks and candy bars to U.S. schoolchildren, who are suffering epidemic levels of type 2 diabetes and obesity. And while commercialism continues to put ads on buildings and buses, in textbooks and at playing fields, a growing number of locales have enacted anticommercialism laws. Such laws limit the transformation of public space into yet more commercial space for corporations, which have succeeded in infiltrating nearly every bit of daily life with advertisements and narratives celebrating consumerism, possessive individualism, social Darwinism, authoritarianism, and a corporate vision for the future of work, leisure, politics, and the environment.

It would be hard to claim that an overwhelming majority of public schools presently facilitate the alternative to corporate culture—that is, democratic culture, or what Dewey called "creative democracy," which requires continual work, practice, and attention to expand a democratic ethos. This is a time of the radical erosion of democratic culture by not only commercial culture but also the state-led dismantling of civil liberties, the resurgence of jingoistic patriotism, and demands for adhesion to a militarized corporate globalization. If many public schools do not foster a democratic ethos necessary for developing in citizens habits of engaged public criticism and participation, the public nature of public schools makes them a crucial "site and stake" of struggle for the expansion of democratic social relations. Public schools harbor a distinct potential for public deliberation that privately owned and controlled educational institutions limit. At stake in the struggle for public education is the value of critical and public education as a foundation for an engaged citizenry and a substantive democracy.

Despite the glaring failures of a number of high-profile public school privatization initiatives, the privatizers have hardly retreated, and in fact they are operating in a far more strategic fashion. The new face of educational privatization could be called "back door privatization"[5] or perhaps "smash and grab" privatization. A number of privatization initiatives are being enacted through a process involving the dismantling of public schools followed by the opening of for-profit, charter, and deregulated public schools. Taken together, these initiatives share a conservative hostility to teachers unions, a hostility to local democratic governance and oversight, and a penchant for "experiments," especially with the private sector.[6] They take guidance from right-wing think tanks and business groups. Four clear yet hardly exhaustive examples for what I am describing are (1) educational rebuilding in New Orleans, (2) educational rebuilding in Iraq, (3) Chicago's Renaissance 2010 project, and (4) No Child Left Behind.

Following the natural disaster of Hurricane Katrina in the U.S. Gulf Coast, a for-profit educational contractor from Alaska named Akima won a no-bid contract to build temporary portable classrooms in the region. But for-profit education's big haul in the Big Easy was in the U.S. Department of Education's imposing the largest-ever school voucher experiment for the region and nation. While New Orleans public schools were not rebuilt for those most in need, a network of charter schools was created for a privileged few. Right-wing think tanks had prepared papers advocating these approaches, describing public school privatization as a "silver lining" and a "golden opportunity" out of the disaster.[7] Such documents discuss strategies to make the temporary voucher scheme permanent and even how to take advantage of future disasters.

In Iraq, the for-profit U.S. corporation Creative Associates International, Incorporated,[8] has made over a hundred million dollars from no-bid contracts with the U.S. Agency for International Development to rebuild schools, develop curriculum, develop teacher training, and procure educational supplies. The company has avoided using local contractors and has spent the majority of funds on security. Educational privatization by Creative Associates International, Incorporated, typifies the way the U.S. invasion has been used to sell off Iraq while furthering U.S. foreign policy in the form of "democracy promotion." Privatization and the development of U.S.-style charter schools are central to the education rebuilding plan (consultants from the right-wing Heritage Foundation have been employed), despite the fact that these are foreign to Iraq's public education system, and members of right-wing think tanks have been engaged to enact what invasion and military destruction have made a lucrative opportunity financially and ideologically.

In Chicago, Renaissance 2010, essentially written by the Commercial Club of Chicago, is being implemented by Chicago Public Schools, a district with more than 85 percent of students who are poor and nonwhite. It will close one hundred public schools and then reopen them as for-profit and nonprofit charter schools, contract schools, and magnet schools, bypassing important district regulations. The right-wing Heartland Institute hailed the plan, saying, "Competition and [public private] Partnerships are Key to Chicago Renaissance Plan," while the president of the Chicago Teachers Union described it as a plan to dismantle public education.[9] These closings are targeting neighborhoods that are being gentrified and taken over by richer and whiter people who are buying up newly developed condos and townhomes. Critics of the plan view it as "urban cleansing" that principally kicks out local residents.[10] Educational privatizers and real estate developers are capitalizing on the human-made disaster of systematic and long-standing public disinvestment in predominantly poor and nonwhite communities.

Likewise, on a national scale, No Child Left Behind sets schools up for failure by making impossible demands for continual improvement. When schools have not made adequate yearly progress (AYP), they are subject to punitive action by the federal government, including the potential loss of formerly guaranteed federal funding and requirements for tutoring from a vast array of for-profit special educational service providers. A number of authors have described how NCLB is a boon for the testing and tutoring companies, while it doesn't provide financial resources for the test score increases it demands.[11] (This is aside from the cultural politics of whose knowledge these tests affirm and discredit.)[12] Sending billions of dollars of support the way of the charter school movement, NCLB pushes schools that do not meet AYP goals to restructure in ways that encourage privatization, discourage unions, and avoid local regulations on crucial matters. One study has found that by 2013, nearly all of the public schools in the Great Lakes region of the United States will be declared failed public schools and subject to such reforms.[13] Clearly, NCLB is designed to accomplish the implementation of privatization and deregulation in ways that open action could not. NCLB is in the business of declaring U.S. public schooling a disaster ripe for privatization.

Whereas "back door" privatization suggests sneakiness, the old "smash and grab" refers to theft. And that is precisely what is being done to public resources. As extensive as corruption is in the Bush administration, the Republican Party, and the corporate sector—as exhibited by a string of corporate scandals and implosions—smash-and-grab schooling is a more systematic result of a particular moment of capitalism.

Contemporary initiatives to privatize public schools can only be understood in relation to the intersections of neoliberal and neoconservative ideology that presently dominate politics.[14] As David Harvey explains, neoliberalism, alternately described as "neoclassical economics" and "market fundamentalism," is an assemblage of economic, political, and cultural policy doctrine. Neoliberalism, which originates with Frederic Von Hayek, Milton Friedman, and the "Chicago boys" at the University of Chicago in the

1950s, redefines individual and social ideals through market ideals. Within this view, individual and social ideals can best be achieved through the unfettered market. In its ideal forms (as opposed to how it is practically implemented), neoliberalism calls for privatization of public goods and services, decreased regulation on trade, loosening of capital and labor controls by the state, and the allowance of foreign direct investment. In the view of neoliberalism, public control over public resources should be shifted out of the hands of the "necessarily bureaucratic" state and into the hands of the "necessarily efficient" private sector. The collapse of the Soviet Union and the end of the Cold War were seized upon by neoliberals to claim that there could be no alternative to global capitalism. Within the logic of capitalist triumphalism, the only course of action would be to enforce the dictates of the market and to expand the market into previously inaccessible places. Public school privatizers in the Gulf Coast, in Iraq, in Chicago, and nationally through NCLB use natural and human disasters to achieve market expansion by pillaging the public sector.

As Harvey explains, the financial record of neoliberalism is not one of success but rather one of failure resulting in crises, instability, and unreconciled contradictions regarding state power.[15] However, as he argues, neoliberalism has been extremely successful at redistributing economic wealth and political power upward. For this reason, Harvey calls for understanding neoliberalism as a long-standing project of class warfare waged by the rich on the rest. Not only have welfare state protections and government authority to protect the public interest been undermined by neoliberalism, but these policies have resulted in wide-scale disaster in a number of places, including a number of countries in Latin America and the Pacific Rim. These disasters have forced governments to rethink neoliberalism as it has been pushed by the so-called Washington consensus. In fact, recent left election outcomes throughout Latin America have largely been a reaction to the neoliberal Washington consensus that imposes neoliberal globalization through mechanisms including the International Monetary Fund (IMF) and the World Bank.

Originally viewed as an offbeat doctrine, neoliberalism was not taken seriously within policy and government circles until the late seventies and early eighties in Thatcher's United Kingdom and in Reagan's United States. As Harvey details, Chile under Pinochet was a crucial testing ground for these ideals, resulting in increased commercial investments in Chile alongside thirty thousand citizen disappearances. The increasing acceptability of neoliberalism had to do with the steady lobbying of right-wing think tanks and electoral victories but also the right conditions, including economic crises that challenged the Keynesian model and Fordist modes of economic production and social formation in the late seventies.[16] Neoliberalism has a distinct hostility to democracy. As Harvey writes,

> Neoliberal theorists are, however, profoundly suspicious of democracy. Governance by majority rule is seen as a potential threat to individual rights and constitutional liberties. Democracy is viewed as a luxury, only possible under conditions of relative affluence coupled with a strong middle-class presence to guarantee political stability. Neoliberals therefore tend to favour governance by experts and elites. A strong preference exists for government by executive order and by judicial decision rather than democratic and parliamentary decision-making.[17]

Such antipathy to democracy in favor of elite governance is endlessly voiced by neoliberal education writers, including members of the Koret Task Force of the Hoover Institution like John Chubb, Terry Moe, Eric Hanuschek, and others.[18] For progressive and critical educators principally concerned with the possibilities for public schooling to expand a democratic ethos and engaged critical citizenry, neoliberalism's antidemocratic tendencies appear as particularly egregious. As the chapters in this book detail, the strategies of dispossession through privatization, deregulation, and commodification of public schooling undermine democratic governance over this crucial public sphere.

In education, neoliberalism has taken hold with tremendous force, remaking educational common sense and pushing forward the privatization and deregulation agendas. The steady rise of privatization and the shift to business language and logic can be understood through the extent to which neoliberal ideals have succeeded in taking over educational debates. Neoliberalism appears in the now commonsense framing of education through presumed ideals of upward individual economic mobility (the promise of cashing in knowledge for jobs) and the social ideals of global economic competition. In this view, national survival hinges on educational preparation for international economic supremacy. The preposterousness of this assumption comes as school kids rather than corporate executives and the structural tendencies of capitalism are being blamed for the global economic race to the bottom. The "TINA" thesis (There Is No Alternative to the Market) that has come to dominate politics throughout much of the world has infected educational thought as omnipresent market terms such as *accountability, choice, efficiency, competition, monopoly,* and *performance* frame educational debates. Nebulous terms borrowed from the business world, such as *achievement, excellence,* and *best practices,* conceal ongoing struggles over competing values, visions, and ideological perspectives. (Achieve what? Excel at what? Best practices for whom? And says who?) The only questions left on reform agendas appear to be how to best enforce knowledge and curriculum conducive to individual upward mobility within the economy and national economic competition as it contributes to a corporately managed model of globalization as perceived from the perspective of business. This is a dominant and now commonplace view of education propagated by such influential writers as Thomas Friedman in his books and *New York Times* columns, and such influential grant givers as the Bill and Melinda Gates Foundation, the richest philanthropy in history.

What is dangerously framed out within this view is the role of democratic participation in societies ideally committed to democracy and the role of public schools in preparing public democratic citizens with the tools for meaningful and participatory self-governance. By reducing the politics of education to its economic roles, neoliberal educational reform has deeply authoritarian tendencies that are incompatible with democracy. Democracy is under siege by neoliberalism's tendency to conflate politics and the public with economics, thereby translating all social problems into business concerns. Yet, democracy is also under siege by a rising authoritarianism in the United States that guts civil liberties and assaults human rights domestically and internationally in the form of the USA Patriot Act, "extraordinary rendition" (state-sanctioned kidnapping, torture, and murder), spying on the public, and other measures that dangerously expand executive power. Internationally, this takes the form of what Harvey has termed "the New Imperialism" and others have called militarized globalization, which includes the so-called war on terror, the U.S. military presence in more than 140 countries, and the encirclement of the world's oil resources with the world's most powerful military. This comes in addition to a continued culture of militarism that educates citizens to identify with militarized solutions to social problems. In education, I have termed this militarism "education as enforcement" that involves enforcing global neoliberal imperatives through numerous educational means.[19]

Harvey offers a compelling economic argument for the rise of repression and militarization, explaining the shift from neoliberalism to neoconservatism: that neoliberal policy was coming into dire crisis already in the late 1990s as deregulation of capital was resulting in a threat to the United States while it lost the manufacturing base and increasingly lost service-sector and financial industry to Asia.[20] For Harvey, the new militarism in foreign policy is partly about a desperate attempt to seize control of the world's oil spigot as lone superpower parity is endangered by the rise of a fast-growing Asia and a unified Europe with a strong currency. Threats to the U.S. economy are posed by not only the potential loss of control over the fuel for the U.S. economy and military but also the power conferred by the dollar's remaining the world currency, with increasing indebtedness of the United States to China and Japan as they prop up the value of the dollar for the continued export of consumer goods. For Harvey, the structural problems behind global capitalism remain the financialization of the global economy and what Marx called "the crisis of overproduction" driving down prices and wages while glutting the market and threatening profits. Capitalists and states representing capitalist interests respond to these crises through Harvey's version of what Marx called primitive accumulation, "accumulation by dispossession."

Privatization is one of the most powerful tools of accumulation by dispossession, transforming publicly owned and controlled goods and services into private and restricted ones—the continuation of "enclosing the commons" begun in Tudor England. If neoliberalism has come into crisis due to the excesses of capitalism (deregulation and liberalization yielding capital flight, deindustrialization, etc.), then the neoconservative response—emphasizing control and order and reinvigorating overt state power—makes a lot of sense. As Harvey explains in *A Brief History of Neoliberalism*, central to the crisis of neoliberalism are the contradictions of neoliberalism's antipathy to the nation and reliance on the state. The neoconservative response to the neoliberal crisis uses national power to push forward economic competition, to pillage productive forces for continued economic growth, and also to control populations through repression as inequalities of wealth and income are radically exacerbated, resulting in the expansion of a dual society of mobile professionals on the one side and everyone else on the other.[21]

There is a crucial tension presently between two fundamental functions of public education for the capitalist state. The first involves reproducing the conditions of production—

teaching skills and know-how in ways that are ideologically compatible with the social relations of capital accumulation. Public education remains an important and necessary tool for capital to make political and economic leaders or docile workers and marginalized citizens, or even to sort and sift out those to be excluded from economy and politics completely. The second function, which appears to be relatively new and growing, involves the capitalist possibilities of pillaging public education for profit, in the United States, Iraq, or elsewhere. It is with this second function of public education for the capitalist state that this book is centrally concerned. Drawing on Harvey's explanation of accumulation by dispossession, we see that in the United States, the numerous strategies for privatizing public education—from voucher schemes, to for-profit charter schools, to forced for-profit remediation schemes, to dissolving public schools in poor communities and replacing them with a mix of private, charter, and experimental schools—follow a pattern of destroying and commodifying schools, where the students are redundant to reproduction processes, while maintaining public investment in the schools that have the largest reproductive role of turning out managers and leaders.

These two strategies of capitalist accumulation, reproduction and dispossession, appear to be at odds. After all, if public schooling is being pillaged and sold off, then how can it reproduce the social order for capital? Yet privatization is targeting those most marginal to capitalist reproduction, thereby making the most economically excluded into commodities for corporations. Hence, EMOs like The Edison Schools target the poor, making economically marginalized people into opportunities for capital the way that for-profit prisons do. Reproduction and dispossession feed each other in several ways: in an ideological apparatus such as education or media, privatization and decentralization exacerbate class inequality by weakening universal provision, weaken the public role of a service, put in place a reliance on expensive equipment supplied by corporations, and justify further privatization and decentralization to remedy the deepened economic differentiation and hierarchization that have been introduced or worsened through privatization and decentralization. The obvious U.S. example is the failure of the state to properly fund public schools in poor communities and then privatizing those schools to be run by corporations.[22] Rather than addressing the funding inequalities and the intertwined dynamics at work in making poor schools, the remedy is commodification and antidemocratic repression.

But public schooling should not be viewed as just a tool of a capitalist state and economy. This is precisely the mistake that neoliberals make in reducing public schooling to its possibilities for individual upward mobility and global economic competitions. Rather, public schooling remains a crucial "site and stake" of struggle for critical forms of public democracy. The most important reason to defend public schools as part of a broader defense of the public sphere is that public schools can be places where engaged and critical citizenship is fostered, where democratic identities can be made, and where democratic culture is forged. The meaning-making activities, the signifying practices of teachers and other cultural workers, matter tremendously as they affirm or contest broader public discourses with material consequences. At this time of expanding authoritarianism, the steady erosion of civil liberties, and the continued amassing of representational power in the realm of corporate meaning-making machinery, the pedagogical task of making critical citizens could not be more crucial to the fate of democracy as an ideal and practical reality. Critical democratic subjects have the capacity to understand claims to truth in relation to the securing of authority and a sense of agency to act with others to challenge the forces that produce oppressive, unjust, and unequal economic, political, and cultural conditions and social relations.

It is crucial to emphasize before turning to what is afoot in New Orleans, Iraq, Chicago, and elsewhere that what Klein terms "disaster capitalism" and Harvey terms "accumulation by dispossession" is not just an economic project involving the redistribution of wealth. Nor is it just a political project involving class warfare and the redistribution of political power. It is also a cultural project.

What Henry Giroux has termed the "cultural pedagogy of neoliberalism"[23] is typified not merely by the language of "silver linings" and "golden opportunities" but also by the turn to business language and models in thinking about the social world, including public school reform and policy. Not only have public school debates been overrun by the aforementioned neoliberal language, but, as we see in New Orleans, business "turnaround specialists" are brought in to dictate school rebuilding, while residents are dispossessed of their communities through economic rationales such as the invocation of "supply and demand" to justify not rebuilding the New Orleans public schools (residents do not return because the schools have not been rebuilt, and then the planners declare that there is no demand for school rebuilding). The idealization of choice, markets, business, deregulation, and antiunionism is propagated in a number of ways through the cultural pedagogy of neoliberalism. It is essential to remember what Pierre Bourdieu emphasized about neoliberalism.

Neoliberal economics ... owes a certain number of its allegedly universal characteristics to the fact that it is immersed or embedded in a particular society, that is to say, rooted in a system of beliefs and values, an ethos and a moral view of the world, in short, an *economic common sense,* linked as such to the social and cognitive structures of a particular social order. It is from this particular economy [that of the United States] that neoclassical economic theory borrows its fundamental assumptions, which it formalizes and rationalizes, thereby establishing them as the foundations of a universal model. That model rests on two postulates (which their advocates regard as proven propositions): the economy is a separate domain governed by natural and universal laws with which governments must not interfere by inappropriate intervention; the market is the optimum means for organizing production and trade efficiently and equitably in democratic societies.[24]

A number of educational forces in addition to schools are required to keep such premises appearing natural and hence unquestionable. Mass media is one of the most powerful pedagogical forces, persistently and relentlessly miseducating the public to understand "the economy" as natural and inevitable. Consider, for example, news programs that report stock prices like the weather; sports that align capitalist values of numerically quantifiable progress and growth with the possibilities of the human body; police shows (nearly half of U.S. TV content) that replace the primary role of the police, protecting private property, with the drama of seldom-committed spectacular murders; the social Darwinist game shows and reality shows that make contestants compete for scarce resources, including money, cut-throat corporate jobs, trophy spouses, and cut-face plastic surgery to compete all the better; or the advertising behind it all that sells the fantasies that comprise a particular kind of radically individualized and cynical consumer view of the self and the social world. Such media products function pedagogically to define what is possible to think and what is impossible to imagine for the future.

Yet, as powerful as mass media is as a pedagogical force, teaching and the traditions of critical pedagogy, critical theory, cultural studies, feminism, progressive education, and critical cultural production offer powerful tools to produce different kinds of visions—hopeful, democratic visions that articulate with growing democracy movements around the world. The neoliberal postulates that Bourdieu denaturalizes appear increasingly dubious at best as wealth and income are radically redistributed upward in the United States and as nation after nation in Latin America rejects the neoliberal Washington consensus in favor of another path that coheres generally much more with the democratic ideals of the global justice movement.[25]

In the chapters that follow, I detail the new form of privatization that works by taking advantage of disaster to push failed conservative privatization initiatives and that undermines democratic governance to do so. In illustrating how these initiatives span domestic and foreign U.S. policy, I encourage readers to recognize that the most crucial matter at stake in debates over privatization and school reform generally is the possibilities for public schooling to expand a democratic ethos and foster democratic practices and social relations with regard to politics, culture, and economy. What is being done for profit and ideology in New Orleans and Iraq, in Chicago and throughout the United States, with NCLB does just the opposite by political dispossession, economic pillage, and cultural symbolic violence. I conclude by calling for pedagogical and material strategies to expand democratic struggles for the public to take back schools, resources, and cultural power as part of a broader democratic alternative to the antidemocratic neoliberal and neoconservative approaches that thrive on disaster and feed on the public.

Notes

1. Naomi Klein, "The Rise of Disaster Capitalism," *The Nation,* May 2005, 9.

2. Staff, "Reading, Writing, and Enrichment: Private Money Is Pouring into American Education—and Transforming It," *The Economist,* January 16, 1999, 55. In academic circles, Paul Hill was striving to make education an investment opportunity. Paul Hill, Lawrence C. Pierce, and James W. Guthrie, *Reinventing Public Education: How Contracting Can Transform America's Schools* (Chicago: University of Chicago Press, 1997). Hill appears at the forefront of calls for Katrina profiteering in 2005, as the first chapter details.

3. See, for example, William C. Symonds, "Edison: An 'F' in Finance," *Business Week,* November 4, 2002, 2, and Julia Boorstin, "Why Edison Doesn't Work," *Fortune,* December 9, 2002, 12. For a detailed discussion of Edison's financial problems and the media coverage of them, see Kenneth J. Saltman, *The Edison Schools:*

Corporate Schooling and the Assault on Public Education (New York: Routledge, 2005).

4. See "Junk King Education," chapter 1 of Robin Truth Goodman and Kenneth J. Saltman, *Strange Love, or How We Learn to Stop Worrying and Love the Market* (Lanham, Md.: Rowman & Littlefield, 2002), for an extended discussion of Milken's educational enterprises.

5. The editors of *Rethinking Schools* describe the federal voucher scheme after Hurricane Katrina as "back door privatization." The Editors, "Katrina's Lessons," *Rethinking Schools* 20, no. 1 (Fall 2005): 4–5.

6. For an important discussion of how neoliberal educational policies destroy democratic public educational ideals, see David Hursh, "Undermining Democratic Education in the USA: The Consequences of Global Capitalism and Neo-liberal Policies for Education Policies at the Local, State, and Federal Levels," *Policy Futures in Education* 2, nos. 3 & 4 (2004): 607–20.

7. For example, Clint Bolick of the Alliance for School Choice described privatization as the "silver lining" of the cloud that was Hurricane Katrina. His op-ed or quote was then carried by countless publications, including the neocon *National Review* and *Heartland Institute* and the *Washington Times, USA Today,* and others. The quote was picked up and repeated by others advocating the same.

8. See the next chapter.

9. For an important scholarly analysis, see Pauline Lipman, *High Stakes Education* (New York: Routledge, 2004).

10. Activist groups include Parents United for Responsible Education, Teachers for Social Justice, and Chicago Coalition for the Homeless, among others.

11. For an excellent collection of criticisms of No Child Left Behind, see Deborah Meier and George Wood, eds., *Many Children Left Behind* (Boston: Beacon, 2004). In relation to what Henry Giroux has called the "war on youth" being waged in the United States, see his important chapter on NCLB in Henry A. Giroux, *Abandoned Generation* (New York: Palgrave, 2003). See also the collection of writings on NCLB on the www.rethinkingschools.org Web site.

12. School rewards professional and ruling-class knowledge and dispositions and disaffirms and punishes the knowledge and

dispositions of working-class, poor, and culturally nondominant groups. See, for example, the work of Antonio Gramsci, Pierre Bourdieu and Jean Passeron, Louis Althusser, Raymond Williams, Michael Apple, Henry Giroux, Jean Anyon, Peter McLaren, Stephen Ball, Donaldo Macedo, Gloria Ladson-Billings, Michelle Fine, Lois Weis, Ellen Brantlinger, and Julia Hall to name just a few.

13. See Edward W. Wiley, William J. Mathis, and David R. Garcia, "The Impact of Adequate Yearly Progress Requirement of the Federal 'No Child Left Behind' Act on Schools in the Great Lakes Region," *Education Policy Studies Laboratory* (September 2005), available at www.edpolicylab.org.

14. Henry Giroux's *The Terror of Neoliberalism* (Boulder, Colo.: Paradigm, 2004) makes a crucial analysis of the cultural pedagogy of neoliberalism. For discussion of neoliberal pedagogy in relation to school curriculum, film, and literary corporate cultural production, see also Goodman and Saltman, *Strange Love.* An excellent mapping of these conservatisms and others can be found in Michael Apple's *Educating the Right Way* (New York: Routledge, 2001).

15. David Harvey, *A Brief History of Neoliberalism* (Oxford: Oxford University Press, 2005).

16. For an excellent succinct discussion of the shift from Fordism to post-Fordism with the rise of neoliberal globalization and the concomitant shifts in social organization and self-regulation, as well as implications for cultural theory, see Nancy Fraser, "From Discipline to Flexibilization? Rereading Foucault in the Shadow of Globalization," *Constellations* 10, no. 2 (2003): 160–71.

17. Harvey, *A Brief History of Neoliberalism,* 66–67.

18. See, for example, Chubb and Moe's neoliberal education bible, *Politics, Markets, and America's Schools* (Washington, D.C.: Brookings Institution Press, 1990). See also the several Koret-edited collections, including *A Primer on America's Schools.*

19. See Kenneth J. Saltman and David Gabbard, eds., *Education as Enforcement: The Militarization and Corporatization of Schools* (New York: Routledge, 2003).

20. Harvey offers important tools for comprehending neoliberalism and neoconservatism in both *A Brief History of Neoliberalism* and *The New Imperialism* (Oxford: Oxford University Press, 2005). However, it is important to note here that these particular books focus heavily on the economic dimensions of neoliberalism

Introduction

and lend themselves to an interpretation that views the material base as prior to the cultural superstructure rather than emphasizing the imbricatedness of culture and materiality. See, for example, the discussion of the brainstorming of the neoliberal architects and the discussion of Gramscian construction of consent in *A Brief History of Neoliberalism*. In these discussions, the ideology of neoliberalism disappears and is repeatedly described as rational planning to redefine such concepts as freedom. What is absent is a sense of how, for example, the public sphere has come to be described and imagined through market language, logic, and dreams. How the stultifying drudgery and authoritarianism of business culture were made into the essence of freedom and even sexiness through consumer culture did not happen because Frederic Von Hayek had sexy thoughts or was sexy or planned with his friends at Mont Pelerin to redefine freedom. In other words, in Harvey's version, cultural production and the ongoing making of meanings and signifying practices are displaced in favor of rational planning. The advantage is that this gives a strong sense of agency to the idea people, but it undercuts the agency of local cultural producers such as teachers or artists whose meaning-making activities and signifying practices enter into and confirm or contest broader public discourses, including neoliberalism and neoconservatism. In addition, the emphasis on rational planning in the formation of ideologies displaces examination of the material conditions within which cultural production takes place at a local level.

21. The expansion of the dual society as a result of neoliberal globalization has been importantly theorized by Zygmunt Bauman, *Globalization: The Human Consequences* (New York: Polity, 1998), and Fraser, "From Discipline to Flexibilization?"

22. See Kenneth J. Saltman, *Collateral Damage: Corporatizing Public Schools—A Threat to Democracy* (Lanham, Md.: Rowman & Littlefield, 2000).

23. Giroux, *The Terror of Neoliberalism*.

24. Pierre Bourdieu, *The Social Structures of the Economy* (Malden, Mass.: Polity, 2005), 10-11.

25. A valuable source for entry into literature on the global justice movement is www.znet.org.

I
Silver Linings and Golden Opportunities

The Corporate Plunder of Public Schooling in Post-Katrina New Orleans

֎

Real estate breeds poetry. Of all creative language, real estate people especially like euphemisms. In the property business, a dark and dingy basement apartment becomes a "garden apartment." "The neighborhood is in transition" means poor people can no longer afford to pay raised rents. Professionals who move into "transitioning" neighborhoods to speculate on rising property values or to pay cheap rent are "urban pioneers." When for years a slumlord charges top rents to tenants who are forced to step around holes in floors and endure broken fixtures, chronic water and gas leaks, missing windows in winter, rats as roommates, and cockroaches as commonplace, such profitable buildings are said to have "deferred maintenance." Deferred maintenance sounds hopeful. The structure may be crumbling, but it can always be fixed, fumigated, painted. It is just a matter of time.

The New Orleans public schools have long been considered some of the most neglected in the United States, suffering not just dilapidated buildings and insufficient resources but all of the ills accompanying malignant poverty, including the deferred maintenance of jobs, deferred maintenance of health care, and deferred maintenance of public and private services. As in the case of most urban school districts, the long-standing linkage of the New Orleans public school funding to the unequal economic hierarchy of the broader economy, and particularly to unequal property ownership, resulted in chronic failure to support this crucial public institution.

Corporate wealth in New Orleans produced shining towers of glass and steel while tourist dollars flowed through restaurants and hotels, bars and sports events, but not to schools. Per-pupil spending in New Orleans as of 1997 was 26 percent below the national average and 16 percent lower than the average of badly underfunded urban school systems nationally.[1] "Public school students regularly had to bring their own supplies to school, from writing paper to toilet paper. The school system was on the brink of financial collapse and struggled to even meet its payroll."[2] As advertising and public relations companies pour billions of dollars a year into marketing junk food, clothing, cosmetics, and other products to youth targeted by race, ethnicity, gender, and class, and as they aim to infiltrate classrooms to hawk product, they and other industries make little effort to shoulder the costs of public services.[3]

The business sector has long failed to support public institutions from which it benefits. In fact, for decades the tax burden has been shifted off business and onto individuals. Under President George W. Bush, these regressive tendencies have radically increased, with the richest Americans who own the majority of corporate wealth receiving massive tax cuts while the middle class has suffered tax increases. Moreover, social spending is being slashed. In 2003, taxpayers making more than $10 million saved $1 million in taxes. "As the Center on Budget and Policy Priorities reports, current and proposed tax cuts for households with incomes above $1 million would cost more than the combined cuts planned over the next five years for education, veterans health benefits, medical research, environmental protection and programs such as housing, energy, child care and nutrition assistance for families living in poverty."[4] The 2006 budget includes $70 billion in new tax cuts for the rich and $35 million in cuts to programs for the least fortunate.[5]

As in Iraq, post-Katrina New Orleans has been seized upon by the Right as a radical free-market experiment in neoliberal privatization and deregulation—a way to undermine the public sphere while strengthening the private sector. *The Guardian* (U.K.) describes the area as a "vast laboratory" for right-wing social policies (in addition to those in education detailed later), including attempts to suspend a series of regulations such as local wage guarantees and affirmative action, as well as environmental regulations, while giving massive tax breaks to business.[6] As this chapter details, disaster is being seized upon and even produced by the political Right to exacerbate inequalities while creating lucrative opportunities for those most well-off.

On August 29, 2005, three massive storm fronts converged, tearing into the Gulf Coast of the southern United States with unprecedented destructive power. Hurricane Katrina splintered houses, flung vehicles, and burst the levees holding back the gulf from the low-lying parts of New Orleans. Floodwaters trapped those who could not afford to evacuate, killing many and stranding without food and water countless others.[7] The incompetence, deliberate or otherwise, of the Federal Emergency Management Agency (FEMA), the White House, and the Department of Homeland Security to properly secure the levees, to provide evacuation means for residents, or to rescue those trapped has been the subject of a vast media spectacle.[8] Briefly, mass media reports focused on the plight of the poor and the racialized nature of poverty in the United States, yet these reports also replicated a deep culture of racism by framing scrounging whites as resourceful heroes and foraging blacks as criminal looters who should be shot on sight. The storm destroyed sizable sections of the low-lying parts of the city inhabited by the poorest, mostly African American, residents. Countless images and narratives of the brutality of the storm and the brutality of the government response have been publicized: elderly residents of nursing homes and hospitals abandoned to drown, corpses left to rot on the front porches of homes, an unidentified corpse left for two weeks in a busy intersection of Bourbon Street. Numerous commentators have proclaimed Katrina the worst urban disaster in U.S. history.[9]

Months after the storm, it became apparent that the scandals of Katrina were hardly limited to the kind of government incompetence and neglect typified by the inaction of Dan Brown, head of FEMA, and Michael Chertoff, head of Homeland Security. Despite presidential praise for FEMA and Homeland Security officials who failed to act ("You're doing a heckuva job, Brownie") and statements after the storm that the tragedy could not have been predicted, video surfaced of President Bush receiving warning of the magnitude of crisis about to unfold. Rather than acting, he went on vacation as the hurricane moved in. Further information arose that in early 2001, FEMA ranked the state of New Orleans' hurricane vulnerability as one of the three most likely disasters, alongside the risk of a terrorist attack on New York.[10] Yet funding to fix the levees had been cut by the Bush administration. The disaster was predicted, and it was preventable.

The storm hit hardest the poorest, predominantly African American residents who lacked the resources to flee its approach after Mayor Ray Nagin called a mandatory citywide evacuation.[11] The city, the state, and the private sector failed to provide transportation to citizens in the line of the storm. Instead, the shelter of last resort was the notorious Superdome, which a study had predicted would not withstand the force of a scale 3 hurricane. The sweltering shelter had not been adequately prepared with provisions as overcrowded, hungry, thirsty people who had just lost all that they owned, their homes and their pets, had no place to sleep. Many died and others suffered without crucial medicine. Some of the bodies of loved ones were lost. For weeks, relatives desperately tried to recover the bodies of those who died in their arms on the floor of the Superdome. Survivors, though spared, felt their lives had been swept away. Hundreds of thousands of residents who had lived their entire lives in

New Orleans were subsequently evacuated to other states. The richest, mostly white, Orleanians were able to return to pricier elevated neighborhoods less impacted by the storm, while the sections of the city worst hit (e.g., the Lower Ninth Ward) remain devastated more than half a year later.

Despite billions of dollars in emergency funding allocated by Congress, the main players in reconstruction—FEMA, the Louisiana Reconstruction Authority (LRA), and the business-oriented Bring New Orleans Back Committee (BNOBC)— have failed to rebuild large sections of the city inhabited by the poorest, mostly black residents. Residents themselves have largely been excluded from the political process of decision making about rebuilding. For residents to return to the city, housing and schools would need to be rebuilt. As Naomi Klein has pointed out, a glut of rental housing sat on the market as residents were forced out of the city. Half of residents could have been housed had they been given housing vouchers by FEMA. These could have worked like Housing and Urban Development (HUD) section 8 vouchers, allowing landlords to receive fair market rent for their units. Instead, those residents who returned to the city were put up in expensive cruise ships and then temporary military barracks–style trailer parks devoid of crucial services and patrolled by private security forces prohibiting basic rights like interviews by journalists. Like the war in Iraq, such decisions seem to have followed from contracting connections rather than public interest. The project of keeping residents from returning to their communities appears in housing policy decisions and school policy as well.

Silver Linings and Golden Opportunities

Six months after the disaster, the destroyed New Orleans public schools sit slime-coated in mold, debris, and human feces, partially flooded and littered with such detritus as a two-ton air conditioner that had been on the roof and the carcasses of dead dogs. "All 124 New Orleans Public Schools were damaged in some way and only 20 have reopened with more than 10,000 students registered. There were 62,227 students enrolled in NOPS before the storm."[12] The devastation nearly defies description. "Katrina roared in, severely damaging about a quarter of the schools: Roofs caved in. Fierce winds blew out walls and hurled desks through windows. Floodwaters drowned about 300 buses. Computers, furniture and books were buried in mud. Dead dogs and rotting food littered hallways."[13]

Yet days after the disaster, the *Washington Times* quoted a long-standing advocate of school vouchers, Clint Bolick of the Alliance for School Choice. Bolick used the tragedy to propose wide-scale privatization of the New Orleans public schools in the form of a massive voucher scheme. He said, "If there could be a silver lining to this tragedy, it would be that children who previously had few prospects for a high-quality education, now would have expanded options. Even with the children scattered to the winds, that prospect can now be a reality—if the parents are given power over their children's education funds."[14] Bolick's metaphor of the silver lining would be repeated over and over in the popular press immediately after the storm, calling for the privatization of the New Orleans public schools. Karla Dial in the *Heartland News* wrote, "Emergency vouchers could be the silver lining in the storm clouds that brought Hurricane Katrina to the Gulf Coast on August 29."[15] Reuters quoted Louisiana state superintendent of education Cecil Picard as saying, "We think this is a once-in-a-lifetime opportunity. I call it the silver lining in the storm cloud."[16] Jack Kemp, who served in the Reagan administration and is a longtime proponent of business approaches to urban poverty, took poetic license but stayed with the theme of precious metal: "with the effort to rebuild after Katrina just getting underway, the Right sees, in the words of Jack Kemp, a 'golden opportunity' to use a portion of the billions of federal reconstruction funds to implement a voucher experiment that, until now, it has been unable to get through Congress."[17] The governor of Louisiana saw gold, too. Although before the storm the state legislature had rejected the governor's attempt to seize control of the public schools from the city,

> legislation proposed by Governor Blanco in November allows the state to take over any New Orleans school that falls below the statewide average on test scores and place it into the state's Recovery School District. Under this low standard, management of 102 of the 115 Orleans Parish schools operating before Katrina would be transferred to the state. The governor sees it as an effort to grasp what she called a "golden opportunity for rebirth."[18]

Brian Riedlinger, the director of the Algiers Charter Schools Association that would control all but one of the reopened New Orleans schools six months after the tragedy, employed a creative variation on the theme, invoking the poetry of Coleridge and the discourse of hygiene. "I think the schools have been a real albatross. And so I think what we're giving parents is the possibility of hope, a possibility of wiping the slate clean and starting over."[19] Two long-standing advocates of public school privatization, Paul T. Hill and Jane Hannaway, carried the hygienic metaphor a step further, writing in their Urban Institute report, "The Future of Public Education in New Orleans," that "education could be one of the bright spots in New Orleans' recovery effort, which may even establish a new model for school districts nationally."[20] This "bright spot," according to Hill and Hannaway, that should be a national model calls for refusing to rebuild the New Orleans public schools, firing the teachers, and, by extension, dissolving the teachers union, eradicating the central administration, and inviting for-profit corporations with sordid histories such as The Edison Schools[21] and other organizations to take over the running of schools.[22]

Sajan George is a director of Alvarez & Marsal, a Bush administration–connected business-consulting firm that is making millions in its role subcontracting the rebuilding of schools. George, a "turnaround expert" contracted by the state, brought these metaphors together by stating, "This is the silver lining in the dark cloud of Katrina. We would not have been able to start with an almost clean slate if Katrina had not happened. So it really does represent an incredible opportunity."[23]

An incredible opportunity indeed.

In what follows, I discuss a number of ways that Hurricane Katrina in New Orleans typifies a new form of educational privatization. I focus on how the disaster has been used to enrich a tiny, predominantly white business and political elite while achieving educational privatization goals that the Right has been unable to achieve before: (1) implement the largest ever experiment in school vouchers; (2) allow for enormous profits in education rebuilding by contracting firms with political connections; and (3) allow the replacement of a system of universal public education with a charter school network designed to participate in the dispossession of poor and African American residents from their communities and to remake the city "cleansed" of former residents. The network described in the third goal is also designed to fire experienced teachers and destroy the teachers union, and destroy the city's public school central office and democratically representative institutions, to replace them with authoritarian and business-controlled bodies and implement the largest experiment with numerous business-oriented school reforms.

In the sections that follow, I address the economic, political, and cultural battles being waged in the wake of Hurricane Katrina through the fights over vouchers, contracting, and charter schools—fights that I argue are ultimately between, on the one hand, the expansion of capital accumulation by pillaging the public sector and dispossessing citizens of their wealth, political power, and cultures and, on the other hand, the possibilities of expanding democratic social relations in terms of politics, economics, and culture. The point in telling the story of how the right wing is taking advantage of disaster to implement democratically failed reforms is to alert readers to how educational privatization and the assault on public schools are taking a new insidious form. Readers are encouraged to work to defend public education as part of the broader struggle for the expansion of democratic social relations and the democratic redistribution of political, economic, and cultural power. I conclude by highlighting the resistance.

Vouchers

Vouchers use public money to pay for private schools and thus stand as a potentially lucrative business opportunity. Right-wing think tanks and advocates of educational privatization have been calling for wide-scale voucher schemes for decades, alleging that the competition for consumers' money will drive up quality and drive down costs. For example, the Heritage Foundation has lobbied for vouchers over many years and published a report immediately after the hurricane calling for vouchers, as did the Urban Institute.[24] Support for vouchers comes largely from the neoliberal ideological belief that applying business ideals to the necessary bureaucratic public sector guarantees efficiencies. Critics of vouchers have contended that (1) encouraging parents to "shop" for schools will take scarce federal resources away from those public schools most in need of them—schools that have historically been underfunded by having resource allocations pegged to local property taxes;[25] (2) vouchers have traditionally been used to maintain or worsen racial segregation in the face of desegregation policies[26]—a particularly relevant legacy to the racial dispossession going on in New Orleans; (3) vouchers undermine universal public schooling by redefining a public good as a private commodity and stand to exacerbate already-existing inequalities in funding; (4) vouchers undermine the public democratic purposes of public schooling by treating citizens as consumers; and (5) vouchers undermine the constitutional separation of church and state.

29

Not only was the voucher agenda being pushed unsuccessfully for years before the storm, but also the only federally funded voucher scheme until Katrina was implemented by the U.S. Congress in the District of Columbia: "one that has been 'marked by a failure to achieve legislatively determined priorities, an inability to evaluate the program in the manner required by Congress, and efforts by administrators to obscure information that might reflect poorly on the program.'"[27] This voucher scheme was snuck through federal legislation by being rolled into a budget bill, and it was aggressively supported by one of the richest people on the planet, Wal-Mart inheritor John Walton of the Walton Family Foundation, one of the largest spenders pushing privatization of public education.[28]

Not only did New Orleans not have a voucher scheme prior to Katrina, but a K–12 voucher bill had been defeated in the Louisiana state legislature just before the hurricane.[29] The bill would have allowed for public tax money to fund private or religious schooling.

Despite public democratic deliberation on the issue concluding against vouchers, conservative privatization advocates moved quickly to take advantage of the disaster. Within two weeks after the hurricane, the Heritage Foundation released a "special report" refashioning its long-standing agenda as "principled solutions" for rebuilding. "Heritage has been pushing school vouchers since 1975 and so it is no surprise that the organization now strongly believes that a voucher proposal that would fund private schools constitutes a successful response to the crisis."[30]

The Bush administration, so slow to provide federal emergency aid to residents, was nonetheless quick to respond to extensive media criticism by formulating help through the privatization proposals of such right-wing think tanks. The administration proposed $1.9 billion in aid to K–12 students with $488 million designated for school vouchers. The editors of *Rethinking Schools* accurately wrote, "This smells like a back-door approach to get public funding for private schools and would essentially create the first national school voucher plan."[31]

Privatization advocates were quite explicit in their desire to undermine local control over educational decision making and to create a situation in which it would be very difficult to reverse the implementation of vouchers. For example, Karla Dial, reporting in the right-wing Heartland Institute *School Reform News,* quotes Chris Kinnan of Freedom Works, a D.C. organization fighting for "smaller government" and more "personal freedom."

> "Having those vouchers for a couple of years would change the way parents and students and even educators think about them," Kinnan said. "The impact would be so powerful that if you did it right, [school] systems would be competing to attract these [kids with vouchers]. It's all about changing the incentive. Once you have that freedom it would be very difficult to go back to the community control system."[32]

For Kinnan and his ilk, "freedom" means privatizing public control over public resources so that fewer people with more wealth and power have more political control over said resources. The genius of framing the amassing of political and economic control over public resources as individual consumer choice is that it takes on the deceptive appearance of increasing individual control, although it actually removes individuals from collective control. Privatizers aim to treat the use of public resources as "shopping" by "consumers," thereby naturalizing the public sector as a market—as a natural, politically neutral entity ruled by the laws of supply and demand rather than as a matter of public priority, political deliberation, and competing values and visions. Such metaphors of consumer culture not only conceal the ways that public goods and services are different from markets (public services aim to serve public interest and collective goals, not the amassing of private profit) but also fail to admit that markets themselves are hardly neutral and natural.

They are, on the contrary, hierarchical, human-made political configurations unequally distributing power and control over material resources and cultural value.

Clint Bolick of the Alliance for School Choice was also scheming to get a foot in the door. Hopeful that the initial one-year period for vouchers in the Bush proposal could be extended indefinitely, he said, "I think that if emergency school vouchers are passed this time they will be a routine part of future emergency relief. I'm also hopeful that when the No Child Left Behind Act is modified that it will be easier for Congress to add vouchers to the remedies available under that law."[33]

The Heritage Foundation, the Alliance for School Choice, and the Heartland Institute were hardly alone as a large number of right-wing groups committed to vouchers praised the president's plan. Gary Bauer of the group American Values hailed the "rebuilding challenge as an opportunity to implement conservative ideas such as school vouchers and tax free zones."[34] The Bush plan was praised by the Family Research Council, Rich Lowry of the *National Review,* Gary McCaleb of the Alliance Defense Fund, Marvin Olasky of *World Magazine,* and William Donohue of the Catholic League, among others.[35]

The Yankee Institute took a full-page color advertisement in Heartland's *School Reform News* with a letter from its executive director, Lewis Andrews, who admonishes readers that when the real estate bubble bursts and public education "cost soars relative to home values" in rich communities, "savvy reformers will be prepared to make the case for school vouchers in all communities."[36] The ad begins with the expression "Every cloud has a silver lining."

Implicit in Andrews's statements is the fact that privatizers have already been taking advantage of the historical failure to properly fund education in poor and working-class communities. Before Katrina, per-pupil spending in New Orleans stood at about $5,000 ($4,986 in 1998). To put this in perspective, per-pupil spending in suburban public school districts in wealthy suburbs around the nation reach as high as roughly quadruple this amount despite the fact that they face far fewer obstacles. As the Right clearly grasps, the question of privatization is inextricably linked to matters of public funding. Vouchers, charters, and EMOs cannot make headway with well-financed public schools in richer communities. Crisis and emergency benefit privatization advocates who can seize on a situation with preformulated plans to commodify this public service. To put it differently, privatizers target those who have been denied adequate public investment in the first place. As the United Federation of Teachers' Joe Derose insists, the policy emphasis in rebuilding should be on the chronic underfunding plaguing the New Orleans public schools rather than on the schemes to privatize them.[37] As the previously cited quotes from Bolick, Kinnan, and Andrews illustrate, the Right is eager to take advantage of crisis to subvert democratic oversight over policy matters of great public importance.

The Bush administration has long aimed to expand vouchers. In 2002, vouchers were removed from the No Child Left Behind bill at the last moment as part of an effort to secure bipartisan support.[38] Not only do the Katrina federal vouchers cover far beyond the Gulf Coast region, but they take advantage of the crisis to promote the idea of vouchers and privatization generally. For example, while select counties and parishes in Alabama, Mississippi, Louisiana, and Florida are included in the emergency impact aid, the entire state of Texas is included in the voucher scheme. While emergency funds do not permit public school rebuilding, they nonetheless give funding to schools in forty-nine states. What is more, the vouchers can be given to charter schools without charter schools meeting section 5210(1) of the Elementary and Secondary Education Act (ESEA), No Child Left Behind, which requires charter schools to be developed with public charter agencies. In other words, the vouchers allow public funding for charter schools that do not need to be held accountable to public oversight institutions that regulate charter schools. As a result, the aid does not merely favor the public funding of private schools. It encourages the development of a disturbing form of privatization—charter schools unregulated by the public sector by funding them when they would otherwise be ineligible to receive federal funding for having failed to meet basic requirements.[39] This is particularly egregious considering the disastrous quality of underregulated experimental schools, such as a number of those created through Milwaukee's voucher experiment.

The emergency aid is also being used to promote and publicize vouchers as a legitimate school reform. As part of the program, the state education agency must provide notice to parents of students attending a nonpublic school, informing them "a. the parent or guardian has the option to enroll his or her child in a public school or a nonpublic school; and b. Emergency Impact Aid is a temporary program that will be available only for the 2005–2006 school year."[40] While at first glance this requirement appears to be about simple notification of policy, in the context of the administration's long-standing push for vouchers, it appears to be designed to encourage parents to support vouchers for private schools in part by emphasizing the withdrawal of resources, albeit in voucher form. Secretary of Education Margaret Spellings made this goal of proselytizing vouchers quite explicit in her speech of April 5, 2006, in a New York church, saying that, in addition to expanding charter schools and the voucher scheme in D.C., "most importantly, we've armed the parents of 48 million public school students nationwide with the information to be smart educational consumers and become real advocates for their children."[41] Spellings notably embraces the neoliberal description of education as a business with consumers rather than as a public good crucial for the making of citizens capable of developing skills and dispositions of self-governance. In this speech, Spellings explains that No Child Left Behind's provision allowing students to attend other schools and its designation of schools as "failed" are designed to expand "choice," which is how she describes both vouchers and the NCLB provision allowing students to go to any school—a measure implemented to set the stage for vouchers. And, as Spellings explains, the voucher scheme in New Orleans is part of an aggressive broader attempt to use federal power to marketize public schooling.

> More than 1,700 schools around the country have failed to meet state standards for five or six years in a row. And many of these schools are in districts where public school choice isn't a real option. We're proposing a new $100 million Opportunity Scholarship Fund to help thousands of low-income students in these schools attend the private school of their choice or receive intensive one-on-one tutoring after school or during the summer.[42]

Immediately after Katrina, Secretary Spellings even sought to waive a federal law that bans educational segregation for homeless children with the obvious purpose of using public funding for private schooling even if explicitly segregated schooling.[43] What is crucial to recognize here is that disasters are being taken advantage of and produced to set the stage for educational privatization. Whether public schools are being systematically underfunded, as were the New Orleans public schools before Katrina, and then declared "failed" (as NCLB is designed to do nationwide), or whether a storm blows them to smithereens does not matter to the privatizers—though the aftermath of Katrina indicates the Right has found just what can be accomplished through sudden massive destruction.

What goes undisclosed in the Department of Education's mandated notification is a comparison of how much money students received in their prior public school relative to the federal funding for the private school. In fact, the vouchers give significantly less money per pupil than New Orleans students received. New Orleans students received an already very low per-pupil funding of roughly $5,000, while Bush's voucher scheme pays only $750 per pupil and then gives money to schools. Clint Bolick argues that a prime reason for vouchers is to save money. Cutting funding for education certainly saves money, but it doesn't explain how educational services are paid for. The numbers don't appear to add up. Congress approved $645 million in the Hurricane Education Recovery Act (HERA), which applies to forty-nine states, and $496 million to the states most severely damaged to reopen schools under the Immediate Aid to Restart School Operations Program (IARSOP). In September 2005, Spellings stated that there were 372,000 schoolchildren displaced from Louisiana and Mississippi. Yet in March 2006, she gave a figure of 157,743 students nationwide who are eligible for a portion of the HERA money as of the first quarter of the year. That would mean HERA should pay about $4,088 per pupil, but schools will receive only $750 per pupil and $937.50 for students with disabilities. Where is the money going? Instead of going to aggressively rebuild the destroyed schools in the regions hardest hit needing the full amount, the money is being dispersed throughout forty-nine states and D.C. "States and the District of Columbia will receive funding under this emergency, one-time program. Funds may be used to hire teachers; provide books and other classroom supplies; offer in-school or outside supplemental services such as tutoring, mentoring and counseling; and cover transportation and health costs."[44] It would be myopic to think that this funding is merely about paying for the new burden of educating hurricane evacuees. This shifting of educational resources around the nation under the guise of emergency needs to be understood in relation to the failure of the Bush administration to pay states' federal funds as part of NCLB. As Monty Neil points out,

> Not only has the federal government failed to meet the social, economic, and health-related needs of many children, but NCLB itself does not authorize nearly enough funding to meet its new requirements. The Bush administration has sought almost no increase in ESEA [Elementary and Secondary Education Act] expenditures for FY2005 and the coming year. The funds Congress has appropriated are about $8 billion per year less than Congress authorized. Meanwhile, states are still suffering from

their worst budget crises since World War II, cutting education as well as social programs needed by low-income people.[45]

It appears that emergency is being used to cover failed promises that have nothing to do with emergency other than the emergencies created by an administration hostile to supporting public education in the first place. But such coverage is taking the form of privatization. Such failures of a conservative executive and legislature to support public education need to be understood in relation to a conservative judicial branch that in 2002 ruled vouchers constitutional. The political Right is waging war on public education while doing all it can to force through privatization initiatives that are unpopular and difficult to win politically.

Neither the HERA nor the IARSOP funds allow money to rebuild the public schools themselves. Without the schools being rebuilt, many residents are not returning to the city. But that seems to be part of the plan of the business-dominated Bring New Orleans Back Commission (BNOBC), the Louisiana Recovery Authority (LRA), the state government, and FEMA.[46] Andy Kopplin, executive director of the governor-formed LRA, made quite explicit state priorities, saying, "Our goal is to try to identify the ways this money can be used to have the most leverage, in terms of providing private sector investment."[47]

Part of why the voucher scheme appealed to business elites in New Orleans and beyond was that, aside from fulfilling a long-standing conservative dream, it participated in removing poor black residents from the city by offering them schooling throughout the Gulf Coast region. As Mike Davis writes,

[Real estate developer–gentrifier] Kabacoff's 2003 redevelopment of the St. Thomas public housing project River Garden, a largely market-rate faux Creole subdivision, has become the prototype for the smaller, wealthier, whiter city that Mayor Nagin's Bring New Orleans Back commission (with Canizaro [a Bush-connected developer] as head of the crucial urban planning committee) proposes to build. . . . BNOB grew out of a notorious

37

meeting between Mayor Nagin and New Orleans business leaders (dubbed by some the "forty thieves") that [James] Reiss [real estate investor and chair of the Regional Transit Authority (i.e., the man responsible for the buses that didn't evacuate people)] organized in Dallas twelve days after Katrina devastated the city. The summit excluded most of New Orleans' elected black representatives and, according to Reiss as characterized in the *Wall Street Journal,* focused on the opportunity to rebuild the city "with better services and fewer poor people."[48]

When the BNOBC faltered in the face of public resistance, they employed the voice of corporate land developers, the Urban Land Institute (ULI). "In a nutshell, the ULI's recommendations reframed the historic elite desire to shrink the city's socioeconomic footprint of black poverty (and black political power) as a crusade to reduce its physical footprint to contours commensurate with public safety and a fiscally viable urban infrastructure."[49] The translation of a land grab into the discourse of safety and security was used to undermine democratic governance over both housing and schooling.

Keenly aware of inevitable popular resistance, the ULI also proposed a Crescent City Rebuilding Corporation, armed with eminent domain, that would bypass the City Council, as well as an oversight board with power over the city's finances. With control of New Orleans schools already usurped by the state, the ULI's proposed dictatorship of experts and elite appointees would effectively overthrow representative democracy and annul the right of local people to make decisions about their lives.[50]

The voucher scheme participated in dispossessing residents of their land and schools to provide profits for investors and remake the city. Contracting initiatives worked in conjunction to achieve the same goals.

These neoliberal public-private initiatives in schooling need to be understood in relation to those that have overtaken housing, military, security, parks, and other public institutions. One of the most relevant in this case is the way that Hope VI public-private partnerships to develop "mixed income" housing have replaced prior public housing around the United States. As with the privatization of schooling, the metaphor of business efficiency stands in for the real ineffi-ciencies introduced through the privatization of public hous-ing as multiple lucrative subsidies for real estate developers, and massive fees for lawyers, come at taxpayer expense while public housing is gutted and poor residents are displaced. Not only do such schemes fail to replace public housing that is dis-mantled, but they also bilk the public of money that could pay for these crucial services while funneling money to the rich. What goes up in place of public housing is gentrified neigh-borhoods populated by richer, whiter residents. This process is being coordinated with the closing of public schools in neighborhoods where public housing is being dismantled. New schools are being opened specifically tailored for the cleansed population, and many of these are charters or other models that opt out of public school district oversight. Renais-sance 2010 in Chicago, as I detail in chapter 3, exemplifies this dispossessive trend, but it can also be found in Portland, Oregon, Boston, and elsewhere. These projects are supported and promoted by business groups like the Metropolitan Plan-ning Council, the Commercial Club, and the Business Round-table. Proponents of such urban cleansing schemes reframe the dispossession of communities as "urban renewal" and trumpet the miraculous achievement of academic success in the newly opened schools (with their new students with more cultural capital), while carefully avoiding discussion of the decimation of public housing and public schools.[51]

Contracting and the Neoliberal Uses of Corruption

In New Orleans, the Gulf Coast, and around the United States following Katrina, the privatizers seized on the tragedy by repeating a tired mantra of long-standing neoliberal argu-ments for vouchers, deregulation, antiunionism, and charter schools. Shifting the question of the public schools onto market logic, they invoked the language of "business failure," "monopoly," "efficiency," and "business turnaround" and wrapped it all in the language of compassion. For example, John Merrow, reporting on public television, describes a dubious program of putting principals in a nine-day training course and then sending them to fix "failing schools." He says, "The newest, hottest idea in education is happening in many states. Borrowing from business, they call these principals turn-around specialists."[52]

The "silver lining" for privatizers was the destruction of a "failed" school system rather than recognizing the extent to which the historical linkage of the public schools to inequalities in wealth and income resulted in what Jonathan Kozol has called "savage inequalities" long before the storm. Privatizers' justifications for vouchers, charters, and contracting are based in market metaphors of market efficiency as superior to the allegedly corrupt public sector. In the media coverage of schooling following Katrina, most journalists and school reformers emphasize a singular theme: the New Orleans public schools had "failed" because they were rife with corruption, and the market will finally bring transparency to school policy and finance. For example, Sajan George and Bill Roberti of Alvarez & Marsal, whose New York–based company was making millions of dollars of public school money as a "turnaround consultant," appeared to lose no opportunity to bash the New Orleans public schools in the press. Their most extreme examples of accounting irregularities were meant to illustrate just how little public control could be trusted to run the schools. These claims appear particularly exaggerated in light of the fact that Alvarez & Marsal was brought in as "turnaround experts" to keep HealthSouth a viable company after a $2.7 billion accounting fraud. In this case, the magnitude of corporate fraud makes the payroll accounting irregularities and unaccounted-for federal funds of the New Orleans public schools look like loose change.[53] While Alvarez & Marsal was happy to work to restore the autonomy of such a profoundly corrupt corporation, there would be no such second chances for the public schools in New Orleans.

What is remarkable in this comparison is that one of the central arguments of educational privatizers is to let public schools "fail" just as businesses do when they are not run properly. As this example shows (as do the examples of WorldCom, Martha Stewart, and, most appropriately, The Edison Schools), corporations are often given second chances and, rather than being allowed to fail, are allowed to offset losses onto shareholders and the government. (The Edison Schools was bailed out by Governor Jeb Bush using the Florida public school teachers' retirement fund money to buy up Edison's failing stock.) Corporate media framed Alvarez & Marsal's work in New Orleans as heroism—fleet-footed corporate America rushed in to rescue Americans from the public itself. Yet, nearly every aspect of the Gulf Coast school rebuilding showcases how profit-motivated actors have been willing to rip off the public sector and undermine the development of universal quality public schooling. This is evident in the cronyism and inflated billing by contractors with ties to the federal government.

Shortly before Hurricane Katrina struck, the state of Louisiana had hired Alvarez & Marsal to work as "turnaround specialists" with the New Orleans public schools. As the predominantly white state government was attempting to seize control from the predominantly African American city schools, they applied a business logic to public schools, treating them as if they were a business that was not profitable rather than as a public service dedicated to acting in the public interest. In a compromise with the state, following the state's attempt to seize the schools, the city school board hired Alvarez & Marsal at a cost of $16.8 million. Rather than recognizing that the city's public schools had been historically underfunded, resulting in a slew of problems such as crumbling infrastructure, low teacher pay, and a lack of adequate services, Alvarez & Marsal determined that the city schools were receiving too much money. Its plan was to cut nearly 10 percent of the system's budget—a cut of $48 million for a school system with a $500 million budget. This was justified as combating corruption. Though the media coverage of the "turnaround" work by Alvarez & Marsal emphasized corruption in the New Orleans schools, it did not include the fact that Alvarez & Marsal has itself been accused of corruption by inflating its contracting fees by 60 percent in work for Bradford Teaching Hospitals in the United Kingdom.[54] Nor did media coverage investigate the relationships of the firm to the Bush administrations and family, including the relationship of director Bill Roberti to the administration of Bush, Sr. (he was appointed by Bush to oversee government *contracting* for military apparel) or the relationship of corporate director David Javdan to George W. Bush (he was general counsel of the Small Business Administration under G. W. Bush and was a legal adviser on federal *contracting* and business development programs for all cabinet departments and federal agencies). Connections and metaphors of business efficiency apparently stood in for experience and credentials with regard to education.

Prior to being hired in New Orleans, Roberti led a team to consult with the St. Louis public schools and admitted having no experience running public schools.

> Roberti freely admits he and his team have no experience or credentials that would qualify them to operate schools. Few, if any, of the ideas that Roberti proposes are new; almost all of them have been tried in piecemeal fashion in other major urban school districts to different degrees and in varying ways. Other districts have privatized departments and outsourced custodial, maintenance or food service. Some districts have closed schools and sold off real estate to save money. What is different in St. Louis is that a new school-board majority, dominated by members backed by Mayor Francis Slay, moved with great haste in ceding operational control to outside consultants.[55]

If what happened in St. Louis sounds familiar, it should. Roberti overstepped the bounds of Alvarez & Marsal's contract, which stipulated noninvolvement in personnel and curriculum decisions, by firing 1,400 teachers.[56] In New Orleans, Alvarez & Marsal's role as "turnaround specialists" took a radical turn with the onset of the hurricane. The *NewsHour* with John Merrow on PBS painted a picture of Sajan George and Bill Roberti heroically trudging through the floodwaters in the middle of the hurricane to rescue personnel files from the central office.

> Katrina not only flooded the schools, but also the central office, where the basic financial and management records—now accurate for the first time in years—were stored on computer disks.
>
> Roberti and George had to rescue those files even though the city was locked down.
>
> BILL ROBERTI: We got through all of the checkpoints, and the first thing we did was we started looking for police. I wasn't going in the school until I knew police officers knew we were there, because I didn't want somebody shooting at us. And we did finally convince a tactical police unit, six officers, to come in with us.
>
> JOHN MERROW: Once they rescued the files, they arranged to pay the nearly 4,000 teachers for their time served before the hurricane. But that was it. Immediately after the storm, the school board put everyone on "disaster leave," and advised teachers to look for jobs elsewhere.[57]

Alvarez & Marsal's heroic directors proceeded to save the documents and fire all of the New Orleans public school teachers. This resulted in the dissolution of the teachers union following a vote by the state legislature to sweep 87 percent of the schools into a state-run recovery district. This annulled the collective bargaining agreement of the United Teachers of New Orleans, which had the exclusive right to negotiate teaching contracts.

Already in place to slash the public school budget before the hurricane, following Katrina, Alvarez & Marsal was in position to take advantage of contracting. They began assessing damage at the public schools and assembling proposals for contractors to put bids in for the work. At the end of February 2006, Mike Thomson of Alvarez & Marsal estimated more than $800 million in physical damage to the schools. Although Alvarez & Marsal in news reports repeatedly alleges to have made terrific progress in straightening out the NOPS financial situation prior to the hurricane, it does not take responsibility for failing to insure the district properly in the event of a storm such as Katrina. FEMA is consequently punishing the schools.

> Thompson estimates the district will be penalized $165 million for under-insuring the school building, and whatever FEMA matches will cost the Orleans Parish School system $55 million for short term emergency repairs. That doesn't count long-term district costs—an estimated $272 million, Thompson said. A & M officials secured a $30 million community disaster loan for the district from the federal government, but NOPS is still looking at a $111 million budget deficit by June 30.[58]

So the school system suffering the most devastating destruction and in most need even before the storm is put in massive debt, underfunding, and rebuilding uncertainty, while Congress distributes nearly a billion dollars in education aid around the nation. More than a year after the storm, the schools have not been rebuilt. To make matters worse, FEMA emergency school contracting in the Gulf Coast appears to be mired in allegations of corruption and cronyism, of which the saga of Alvarez & Marsal is but one part.

Friends at FEMA: Akima's No-Bid Contract

FEMA is under the Department of Homeland Security (DHS). Homeland Security's first secretary under George W. Bush was Tom Ridge. Tom Ridge, former governor of Pennsylvania, has a history of working to have a mostly white state government seize a mostly black city school district in the case of Philadelphia, to then turn the schools over to be run for profit by a company with a dubious financial and performance record, The Edison Schools.[59] Ridge is a magnet for coincidence. While at DHS, he presided over the regular issuance of scare warnings in the form of color-coded terror alerts that coincidentally escalated throughout Bush's reelection campaign and ended when Bush won his second term. Ridge left DHS at the end of Bush's first term to work as a lobbyist for Blank Rome Government Relations, a lobbying firm whose CEO is David Girard-diCarlo, coincidentally a fund-raiser for Tom Ridge.[60] On Ridge's first day on the job at DHS, he flew out to Girard-diCarlo's home in Scottsdale, Arizona. There is extensive investigative journalism on the relationships between Ridge and many companies that received DHS contracts throughout Ridge's time there. No ethics rules in the newly formed department prohibited what would be conflict of interest in most government departments. Ridge disclosed investments he made with companies doing business with DHS ranging between $100,000 and $800,000 while he was still with the department. Shortly after resigning in 2005, Ridge appeared on *The Daily Show* with Jon Stewart and explained his decision to enter the private sector as being partly about the need to make money to pay for his children's education.

Immediately following Katrina, DHS gave an Alaska-based company called Akima a $40 million no-bid contract to build portable classrooms in Mississippi. Akima, which has a mix of twenty-six no-bid and competitive federal contracts, is majority owned by Nana Regional Corporation, "which coincidentally happens to be a client of Blank Rome Government Relations, a lobbying firm with close ties to the Bush administration and former head of the Department of Homeland Security Tom Ridge."[61] Other Blank Rome employees include high-ranking DHS officials under Ridge, Mark Holman and Ashley Davis (a Ridge staffer who worked on both Bush campaigns). Nana officials and employees donated thousands of dollars to Republican Congress members from Alaska.[62]

Representative Bennie Thompson (Miss.) wrote to the DHS inspector general charging that the government is paying $88,000 for each mobile classroom when a local Mississippi company can provide them for a market rate of $42,000. This would mean that more than half of the $40 million emergency funds allocated by FEMA were being expropriated out of state through these connections while a local firm that could do it for less than half was dropped from consideration.[63] The General Accounting Office (GAO), the investigative branch of Congress, investigated and concluded that the negotiated prices were indeed inflated. Thompson explained that the deal made no sense because FEMA could have hired the local business directly. Instead, Akima subcontracted the work and took a massive cut. By mid-November 2005, Akima's original bid of $40 million was up to $72 million, allegedly because of the need to do additional work. However, even the installation of the modular classrooms appeared to be done in a questionable cost-cutting fashion. Rather than following the Mississippi Board of Education code and pouring concrete foundations with steel posts to anchor the structures, Akima had the units tethered with straps to anchors that had been drilled into the ground. The president of Akima, John Wood, denied "gouging the government" but refused to divulge how much profit the company made on the deal.[64]

In the press, much was made of the fact that Akima secured its no-bid contract by having a minority business status due to the fact that it has 20 percent native Alaskan ownership. However, the rules do not require the company to be managed by native peoples, and Akima is not. Cultural difference in the form of indigenousness in this case appears to have served the interests of securing profits for businesspeople nonindigenous to the region in question while dispossessing work for those who live in the disaster area. Cultural difference was used as a tool to grab inflated contracting through inside connections to a federal government and Republican party riddled with corruption scandals, from the lobbying scandals of Tom DeLay and Jack Abramoff (who also took advantage of minority status legislation) to the tangled web of lies used to justify the invasion of Iraq and discredit its critics.

The subversion of local business in Mississippi was part of a larger pattern in New Orleans. As Mike Davis points out, the loss of local construction contracts by African Americans was systematic and planned from the top.

Even more egregious was the flagrant redlining of black neighborhoods by the Small Business Administration (SBA), which rejected a majority of loan applications by local businesses and homeowners. At the same time, a bipartisan Senate bill to save small businesses with emergency bridge loans was sabotaged by Bush officials, leaving thousands to face bankruptcy and foreclosure. As a result, the economic foundations of the city's African-American middle class (public-sector jobs and small businesses) have been swept away by deliberate decisions made in the White House. Meanwhile, in the absence of federal or state initiatives to employ locals, low-income blacks are losing their niches in the construction and service sectors to more mobile outsiders.[65]

Accusations of a corrupt, predominantly black school system by a predominantly white state and federal government that appears to be more corrupt and at a higher level highlight a deep alignment of neoliberal ideology with white supremacy. The theme of corruption of the public sector and the efficiency of the private sector thrives on a legacy of racist and colonial thought that aligns whiteness, economic power, and the state with the historical discourses of civilization, technological mastery, rationality, planning, order, science, control, the mind, discipline, masculinity, and universality. The other side of these discourses of power is their opposite, frequently ascribed to subaltern populations: savagery, primitivism, irrationalism, presentism, disorder, nature, the body, indiscipline, laziness, femininity, and difference. Within an array of cultural meanings, allegations of corruption can be selectively mobilized within representations such as the spectacle of Katrina to link up with a number of other assumptions attributed to particular populations. Hence, while Alvarez & Marsal has inside connections to the White House and a questionable past for inflated contracting, and while Akima, FEMA, and Homeland Security have indulged in what is hard to call anything other than corruption, these businesses and state agencies working for the benefit of businesses are represented in corporate media as saving the New Orleans public schools from their corrupt past. Such inversions are intertwined with racial politics that represent nonwhites as incapable of self-governance; that represent whiteness as aligned with civilization, progress, efficiency, and discipline; and that link up with representations of business as ideally managing the social scene and determining public priorities. In New Orleans, these cultural politics played a large role along with neoliberal ideology and corruption to dispossess poor, working-class, and nonwhite residents of public schools and homes. This was achieved by framing as common sense such remedies as refusing to rebuild the New Orleans public schools and instead engaging in one of the most radical experiments in public school privatization ever.

Seizure

The failure to rebuild the public schools was intimately linked to attempts to dispossess residents of their homes, work, and communities. Shortly after the hurricane, the BNOBC came up with its notorious "four month plan" that prohibited residents from returning to their communities while requiring these prohibited residents to apply to a citywide planning body with a recovery plan that would need to be approved to return to their homes.[66] After four months, the areas in question that hadn't met the nearly impossible conditions would have their communities bulldozed and taken over by developers. Former New Orleans mayor

Marc Morial, who is president of the National Urban League, described the plan as a "massive red-lining plan wrapped around a giant land grab."[67]

Although the four-month plan was beaten back, the schools were nonetheless successfully seized by the state. All but 15 of the 117 schools in the system were taken over, and all but one are operating as charter schools. The storm also set the stage for political dispossession. As Ronald Utt of the Heritage Foundation put it, gloating over the political implications of the storm, "The Democrats' margin of victory is living in the Astrodome in Houston."[68] As Mike Davis argues, the implications extend far beyond the city. "Thanks to the Army Corps's defective levees, the Republicans stand to gain another Senate seat, two Congressional seats and probably the governorship."[69] With regard to schools, Sharon Cohen puts it, "Some see post-Katrina changes as a move to shift education policy to the right and further undermine its struggling schools."[70] Despite being a Democrat, Governor Blanco used the disaster to slash public spending by $500 million, give tax breaks to oil corporations on the basis of economic development, and take the schools. Supported by rural conservatives, she fended off a challenge by the Legislative Black Caucus to her actions that sidestepped lawmakers.[71]

The state clearly refused to rebuild more in accordance with the business visions of the BNOBC. "Before Katrina hit August 29, the New Orleans district served 56,000 students. Currently, it's handling nearly 10,000 students with a capacity for 2,000 more, according to the state."[72] The United Teachers of New Orleans (UTNO) disputes the state's claims about capacity and sued to force the city to open more schools. Joe DeRose of the UTNO said, "Not enough schools are being reopened and kids are being denied access," emphasizing that the charter schools are hiring unqualified teachers to save money and capping low salaries.[73] The union's charge that too few schools are being reopened was confirmed by the head of the Algiers Charter Schools

Association, who said, "There are not enough schools open in New Orleans and we're trying to fix that problem."[74] "The union disputes the state's capacity numbers, claiming there are more students than space. Union leaders also argue that by returning soon to a larger school district, the city will be able to lure more citizens with a sense of normalcy."[75] But that does not appear to be what the planners want. Instead, they have forced a radical school model that deregulates the central administration, dismantles the union, and shifts power away from public control to a small number of business-oriented leaders. As USA Today reported, reopening the New Orleans public schools would threaten the radical experiment. "If state education leaders are allowed to lay out their plan deliberately, in years to come Los Angeles, Detroit, and other cities with troubled schools will come to New Orleans to learn valuable lessons. Opening schools for the sake of opening schools, however, would only compromise that dream."[76]

Charters

Following the state seizure and dismantling of the New Orleans public school system, the BNOBC endorsed an education plan that breaks the New Orleans school district into "clusters" of eight to fourteen schools.[77] The network clusters would have near-total control of curriculum decisions, budgets, hiring and firing of teachers, and length of the school day, among other decisions that had been district-wide policy. Breaking up the system into semiautonomous clusters will mean that housing quality and price will more closely correspond to school plans by shifting power over schooling in a radically localized way. Put differently, the plan ensures the exacerbation of the most unequalizing effects of schools being tied to property values.

In the last month of 2005, the stripped-down school board would retain control of only eight schools in a system that had been composed of 120. The state of Louisiana took control of roughly 90 percent of the schools—102 of 117 public schools—on the grounds that they had failed to meet academic standards.[78] The state-seized schools comprise the Louisiana Recovery School System, and fifteen schools were made into an independent network of charter schools run by the Algiers Charter School Association. The state seizure that was done in Louisiana (which was also done in Philadelphia and is being fought out in Baltimore as I write) needs to be understood as precisely what No Child Left Behind is designed to do around the United States, which, as in Louisiana, stands to undermine democratically elected school boards, dismantle unions, dismantle schools, and shift power to centralized bodies heavily influenced by business.

What is confusing yet crucial to grasp is that *federal and state power is being used to radically localize control over schooling yet in ways that do not increase local democratic control.* This shift is exemplified by taxpayer succession movements by rich neighborhoods in Los Angeles and New York that aim to segregate economically and racially the enclaves of privilege from urban areas, thereby allowing rich citizens to hoard public resources.

This individualizing and antipublic trend is also exemplified by the Supreme Court's landmark 2005 decision (*Kelo v. City of New London*) that allows locales to seize private property for the purposes of economic development. Previously, eminent domain had to be justified on the basis of public interest, but the new ruling redefines the public interest through economic development. For example, a residential neighborhood designated as suffering "blight" (and this is a hotly contested designation) can be bulldozed, and the land can be seized by the city. Rather than being put to public use (parks, schools, etc.), the land then can be handed over to private developers, for example, to put up a shopping mall. In her dissent, Justice Sandra Day O'Connor pointed out that such a redefinition of eminent domain would inevitably result in larger, more powerful businesses using local political power to gobble up smaller ones.

In this case, the neoliberal redefinition of the public interest through business interests undermines not only the public interest but also the possibility for genuine market competition. In the case of the New Orleans public schools, the federal government and the state orchestrated the radical localizing of control. As Louisiana state superintendent of education Cecil Picard admitted, replacing the public school system with charters was the most expedient approach because "federal dollars were immediately available for them."[79] Pumping massive federal funds into the charter school movement, No Child Left Behind made the dismantling of public schools and the opening of charter schools an intelligible choice. In a sense, then, the implications of New Orleans' radical restructuring can be understood as No Child Left Behind on steroids.

However, before conclusions are drawn about the results of the plan, it must be recognized just how much the plan has been involved in dispossessing residents of public services and political control, and in the extent to which the seizure of the schools is inseparable from the dispossession of residents from their communities. In April 2006, Betty DiMarco, a member of Community United to Reform Education (CURE), demanded the opening of schools at a public meeting, stating, "There are a few schools open in uptown New Orleans. There are a few schools open in Algiers. Those families who have returned in the Treme and Central City area do not have schools to attend."[80] William Giles, a veteran teacher, reported hundreds of students wandering the city streets despite "at least 10 to 20 schools that can be open within three weeks that have only minor damage."[81] The press thinly veiled white middle-class hopes to use the hurricane to "retake control" of the schools. Before Katrina, middle-class, mostly white parents abandoned the city schools for private schools, resulting in segregation. They removed their political clout from the public schools and then blamed the abandoned school system for what a legacy of racism and classism had bestowed on it.[82]

Although charter schools comprise about 4 percent of public schools nationwide, the New Orleans plan gives them a much bigger role. This comes despite mixed to poor reviews of charter performance conventionally determined. In 2004, the *New York Times* reported on the release of National Assessment of Educational Progress (NAEP) scores showing that charter schools are less likely to meet performance goals than comparable public schools. This ignited a firestorm of reaction by conservative charter school advocates, and the Department of Education subsequently altered such reporting to avoid damaging truths from getting out to the public. The Economic Policy Institute published one of the most comprehensive and careful analyses of charter-to-public comparisons and found "evidence that the average effect of charter schools is negative."[83]

Although the implications are no small matter for a reform that is being forced into place without public oversight, my concern is less with the insufficient "delivery" of educational services than with the ways that the charter school movement is part of a broader privatization movement designed to undermine public goods and services in order to pillage and commodify them. Moreover, such undermining of the public sector in this way undermines the capacities for public institutions to be sites of democratic deliberation and transformation. According to the Educational Policy Studies Laboratory at Arizona State University, for-profit schools represent the fastest-growing sector of charter schools, suggesting that charter schools should be understood as a central aspect of the privatization movement. What is more, once control has been wrested from school districts and districts are weakened, it will be easier for charter schools to be taken over by for-profit companies, and the democratic possibilities for such schools will be further imperiled.

In what follows, I focus on two aspects of the radical new model in New Orleans: (1) bad justifications for the plan based on the need for flexibility in a time of uncertainty, and (2) the extent to which an ideology of corporate culture drove the plan.

In a strictly practical sense, unions, school boards, and district offices play crucial roles in maintaining public oversight, ensuring a stable and reliable workforce with relatively low teacher turnover; protecting teacher salaries and benefits; providing certified teachers and educated and competent administrators capable of public management; and working to ensure stable, reliable, and secure systems. As I have detailed in my book *The Edison Schools,* when Philadelphia was seized by the state and The Edison Schools took over a number of schools (about half of Edison schools are charters), this move had dire implications for teacher turnover rates, financial accountability, public oversight, teacher experience, and school culture.

Charter schools are plagued by uncertainty and insecurity because they typically do not have many of the guaranteed features that regular public district schools have, including physical sites, transportation, meals, and steady income. Charter schools are heavily reliant on philanthropic organization and grant writing, which means that funding support can dry up at any time. Much has been made by charter school proponents of the inventive new models that can be devised with the flexibility of the charter school ideal.[84] The problem with this perspective is that while in theory charter schools could lend themselves to offering emancipatory alternatives to the public school system, the development of charters weakens the struggle to make emancipatory public schools while also being constrained by the real limits charter schools have to work within. For example, they are subject to funding constraints and corporate philanthropy that push them toward conservatizing choices regarding curriculum, school model, and so forth, such as the embrace of standardized measures of achievement. The forms of the schools will tend to correspond to the predilections and constraints of funders and the trends of the moment—especially the trend of privatization. As a leading researcher of charter schools, Amy Stuart Wells, writes,

> It is clear that charter schools have gained a great deal of autonomy in terms of private fund raising, including and excluding children, and hiring and firing employees. In these ways, they look more like private than public schools, which is no doubt the intent of free-market reform advocates who see charter schools as one step down the path to full-blown voucher programs.... We see from our study and many others that charter schools are not held any more accountable than other public schools for student achievement. And similar to the growth in income inequality in general over the past 20 years, the gap between the rich and the poor is only exacerbated under charter school reform.[85]

It is no coincidence that charter schools are being strongly promoted in cities by corporations and business groups such as the Commercial Club and Business Roundtable. A leading cheerleader for privatization, Paul T. Hill (whose Urban Institute report reads like a blueprint for the New Orleans plan), emphasized that the city should not invest in rebuilding schools because of uncertainty about students' neighborhoods. Hill and coauthor Jane Hannaway make the bad argument that the rebuilding model is justified on the basis that the future of New Orleans rebuilding is uncertain, and so a "flexible" model is beneficial. In fact, the report and the "flexible" model, which keeps the public school system from being rebuilt, participate in producing uncertainty and insecurity about the future by failing to provide a crucial feature of public infrastructure necessary for residents to return. As Sharon Cohen reports for the Associated Press, "The need for charter schools to take responsibility for services once provided by the school boards, such as food and transport, is an extra burden that some new schools could find 'overwhelming.'"[86]

To deal with this potentially overwhelming extra burden, where did the charter schools turn? To businesspeople. The

Rex Organization established "Project Purple" to match member business skills with the eleven new charter schools that lack these particular administrative skills.[87] In fact, press coverage about the charter school openings reveals how the new model is about closing public schools and opening schools like businesses. Many who embraced the assumption that schools are like business and the rhetoric and metaphors of market efficiencies had a rude awakening.

> "You don't realize that you're starting a business, and the business is public education, but there were all these services that were provided, not efficiently, by the school system," she said. "I think that we got into this charter-school notion because the public schools weren't doing well, but there's no guarantee that because you're a charter school, you're going to do well." McPhee's epiphany has been common among people who are experiencing heavy doses of reality after their initial idealistic eagerness to form charter schools in the belief that they would do a better job of educating their children.[88]

The Project Purple volunteers, who are mostly corporate employees, speak of public schools entrepreneurially, describing the need to build business skills in a school staff that has been gutted of knowledgeable public administrators. In place of the central office, Project Purple pushes business volunteerism. Of course, the communities that will benefit from this are those communities populated by residents with the time and knowledge to contribute to their schools. As a result, such deregulation inevitably results in exacerbated inequalities in resource distribution with regard to administration.

The corporate model of the new school plan extends the authoritarian structure and tendencies of the corporation into the school format.[89] This resulted in the most hierarchical form of school governance, with the head of the Algiers Charter School Association handpicking principals, who in turn would handpick teachers and have total control and authority over every aspect of the school. The district policies and procedures were simply thrown out by the charter association. The power of the principal unilaterally to hire and fire staff and the defiance of unionization are central to the new model. John Merrow interviewed one principal, John Hiser, who said, "I can hire and fire. In fact, I was telling the teachers yesterday that we are all accountable, that I will determine whether they stay or whether they go. They will determine whether I stay or whether I go."[90] In fact, while Hiser can determine whom to hire and fire, it will be test scores that will generally determine whether he will be retained by the person who runs the Charter Association. Consequently, Hiser will have an institutional incentive to do anything he can to effect that end, whether it means threatening teachers' job security or forcing teachers who are no longer protected by their union to work longer unpaid hours. Such a high-pressure system can be profoundly counterproductive, as it was with The Edison Schools, resulting in high teacher turnover, walkouts, or slowdowns and cheating on tests to meet constantly rising expectations.[91]

Centralized authority has long been a call of conservative privatization advocates such as the Hoover Institution, which often blamed the failures of The Edison Schools to succeed on governance and accountability being shared.[92] However, the case of New Orleans highlights some of the dire limitations of such narrow accountability. The new structure removes deliberation and dialogue from the process of administration. As one teacher complained, "once the [charter school association] hands down a decision, that's the way it is."[93] Henry Shepard, a principal of Harte Elementary School, spoke out critically in *Education Week* of the concentration of control over the hiring process. "'I don't like being the one that picks teachers,' he said. 'I think it should be a committee, that I'm part of, [that picks].'"[94] Shepard's perspective certainly makes more sense than the dubious method of hiring that the Algiers Charter School Association used under the direction of its leader, Brian Riedlinger.

Six hundred people, who ranged from certified teachers to a baker, applied for the roughly 150 teaching positions in the Algiers system. After a 10-minute interview with each applicant, 250 were called back. The applicants were then asked to write a one-paragraph statement about teaching, which was graded by a college professor, and answer five 8th grade mathematics problems.[95]

The corporate model extends from concentrated governance resulting in shoddy hiring practices to the downward pressure on smaller units within the structure to do more with less. With the central office gone, "administration would be pared to a minimum. A 'services group' would provide financial, transportation, and other key services. A 'strategy group'—the CEO and a handful of other employees—would be in charge of academics, finances, accountability, and communications."[96] Though initially the plan would have ended the democratically elected school board, it was later amended to be constituted by a mix of elected and appointed members. Such de-democratizing of the school board to ensure state-appointed representatives was engineered in part through the pushing of Scott Cowen, president of Tulane University and head of the education committee of the BNOBC, and Mark Hoffman of Boston Consulting Group, who coordinated the committee. In keeping with the conservative tradition of authoritarian governance models, Hoffman said that "one single, aligned governing body" was crucial to the success of the new model. Yet, as Catherine Gewertz wrote, "Exactly how to ensure such governance in a district where most of the schools will answer to state-contracted groups, and a minority will answer to the local board, is unknown, Mr. Hoffman acknowledged."[97]

The new structure appeals to privatization advocates like Hill and Hannaway because it sets the stage to contract out running schools to for-profit companies. They make this agenda explicit. "To attract school providers with national reputations and track records for developing functioning schools quickly, the city might turn to the likes of KIPP,

Edison, Aspire, and National Heritage Academies."[98] They advocate luring these companies, with at best questionable records of performance, by handing over publicly rented space and giving them "significant freedom in spending and teacher hiring." In a footnote after praising Edison for "quality control and disclosure" (both of which, in fact, have extensive documented problems),[99] they state that Edison's "results are mixed" and direct readers to the Rand report that—they fail to mention—Edison itself commissioned and paid for.[100] This Rand report was delayed from release repeatedly only to be finally issued after Edison's stock was bought up with public school teacher retirement funds.

The ideology of corporate culture has been invoked to justify the refusal to rebuild the public schools. In the first month of 2006, state superintendent Picard denied the interests and politics playing out in New Orleans and justified the schools' remaining unbuilt and undercapacity by claiming, "This [rebuilding] is all driven by supply and demand."[101] "Turnaround specialists" Sajan George and Bill Roberti also used the supply-and-demand metaphor in an interview with John Merrow.

> SAJAN GEORGE: The school system will have a major influence on whether this is a childless city. A lot of these kids are in good school systems in other cities. Why would you pull them out of that? But if you start building a school system that will make a difference and that is not only a good New Orleans system, good school system, but good system for the country, we won't be childless.
> JOHN MERROW: If you build it, they will come?
> BILL ROBERTI: We believe that's right.
> SAJAN GEORGE: That's right.

Of course, Merrow, George, and Roberti are referring to the Kevin Costner fantasy film *Field of Dreams* in which a man builds a baseball field in the middle of farmland, resulting in the miraculous appearance of the ghosts of great dead ball players. Costner's character hears a voice in his head saying,

"If you build it, they will come." The film is a lamentation on the reduction of the dreams for the social world to the limits of economic reality of supply and demand. It portrays a fantasy of defying economic considerations in favor of un- leashed desire. In the context of the interview, this reference is more than a little perverse, especially when the rebuild- ing of New Orleans is being dictated by the urban cleansing dreams of an economic and racial elite. On another level, the film is an apt neoliberal metaphor for those who want to capitalize on disaster: now that the storm has done the clear-cutting, the dream of the field of economic competition can be built. At least that is the fantasy.

Conclusion

Public school privatization threatens the possibility for public schools to develop as places where knowledge, peda- gogical authority, and experiences are taken up in relation to broader political, ethical, cultural, and material struggles informing competing claims to truth. Struggles against these ideologies and their concrete political manifestations must link matters of schooling to other domestic and foreign poli- cies. It is incumbent on progressive educators and cultural workers to imagine new forms of public educational projects and to organize to take back privatized educational resources for public control.

Such struggles are ongoing in New Orleans. As the editors of *Rethinking Schools* write, "There is no silver lining to a disaster like Katrina, but where there is resistance there is hope."[102] They have taken the initiative to propose ways that educators can support groups that are fighting to rebuild public schools, stop the gentrification of communities, implement public oversight over rebuilding, and challenge the multiple forms of antidemocratic apartheid, educa- tional apartheid, and also the many other forms apartheid takes, including racial, economic, employment, health care, housing, and transportation. Organizations struggling in

New Orleans include Community Labor United, Quality Education Is a Civil Right, PURE, and ACORN. Readers can find crucial information from their Web sites as well as from groups that have gone to great lengths to highlight the social justice struggles central to Katrina: New York Collective of Radical Educators (NYCORE), rethinkingschool. org, zmag.org, commondreams.org, and Teachers for Social Justice.

In conjunction with activism, it is incumbent on educators to theorize the democratic implications of schooling in disaster capitalism. As this chapter has demonstrated, the political right is aiming to subvert democratic control over public schooling in terms of policy, school structure, and model. Katrina itself can be the basis for critical lessons, and a number of progressive educators are already developing such curriculum. New and more aggressive forms of taking back public institutions build on critical pedagogies.

The next chapter attempts to expand the possibilities for theorizing the present political moment by detailing how the political Right is using the language of "democracy promotion" to undermine democratic participation and democratic culture as part of the strategic aims of U.S. foreign policy that acts on behalf of an emergent transnational capitalist class. What emerges are startling overlaps in the ways that disaster capitalism is being used by the Right for educational profiteering.

Notes

1. Orleans Parish School Board, "BGR Outlook on Orleans," available at http://www.bgr.org.

2. Sharon Cohen, "New Orleans' Troubled Schools Get Overhaul," Associated Press, March 4, 2006.

3. Businesses do, of course, exploit such underfunding of public services by promising cash in exchange for a captive market for products. See Alex Molnar, *School Commercialism* (New York: Routledge, 2005).

4. Holly Sklar, "Warning Tax Cuts for the Rich Harm the Nation's

Health," Znet Commentary, April 28, 2006, available at http://www.zmag.org.

5. Judd Legum, Faiz Shakir, Nico Pitney, Amanda Terkel, Payson Schwin, and Christy Harvey, "Budget: After Katrina, More of the Same," ThinkProgress.Org, October 21, 2005, available at http://www.americanprogressaction.org.

6. Julian Borger, "Hurricane Aid Used 'To Test Rightwing Social Policies'," *The Guardian,* September 22, 2005, available at http://www.commondreams.org.

7. The questions raised by Hurricane Katrina are numerous, and much that is utterly central to serious inquiry is beyond the scope of this chapter. But it is important to emphasize that such matters as militarized neoliberalism, systemic racism, and the disastrous results of global warming as an effect of global capitalism are as much the story of schooling in disaster as the matter of privatization of the public sector.

8. For a brilliant discussion of the spectacle of Katrina, see Henry A. Giroux, *Stormy Weather: Katrina and the Politics of Disposability* (Boulder, Colo.: Paradigm, 2006).

9. Gary Rivlin, "New Orleans Commission to Seek Overhaul of Schools and Transit," *New York Times,* January 11, 2006, A1.

10. Sidney Blumenthal, "No One Can Say They Didn't See It Coming," Salon.com, August 31, 2005, available at http://www.salon.com. See also Paul Krugman, "A Can't Do Government," *New York Times,* September 2, 2005.

11. For two important discussions of the politics of race and Hurricane Katrina, see Michael Eric Dyson, *Come Hell or High Water* (New York: Perseus, 2006), and Giroux, *Stormy Weather.*

12. April Capochino, "More Than 100 N.O. Schools Still Closed," *New Orleans City Business,* February, 27, 2006, available at http://www.neworleanscitybusiness.com.

13. Cohen, "New Orleans' Troubled Schools Get Overhaul."

14. Clint Bolick, "Katrina's Displaced Students," *Washington Times,* September 15, 2005, http://www.washtimes.com/op-ed/20050914-091903-7385r.htm.

15. Karla Dial, "Emergency School Vouchers Likely for Katrina Victims," *Heartland Institute School Reform News,* November 2005, available at http://www.heartland.org.

16. Cohen, "New Orleans' Troubled Schools Get Overhaul."

17. People for the American Way, "Hurricane Katrina: A 'Golden

Opportunity' for the Right-Wing to Undermine Public Education," November 14, 2005, available at http://www.pfaw.org.

18. Paul Hill and Jane Hannaway, "The Future of Public Education in New Orleans," in *After Katrina: Rebuilding Opportunity and Equity into the New New Orleans* (Washington, D.C.: Urban Institute, January 2006).

19. *Online NewsHour,* "Rebuilding New Orleans Schools," December 19, 2005, available at www.pbs.org/newshour/bb/education.

20. Hill and Hannaway, "The Future of Public Education in New Orleans."

21. See Kenneth J. Saltman, *The Edison Schools: Corporate Schooling and the Assault on Public Education* (New York: Routledge, 2005).

22. Hill and Hannaway, "The Future of Public Education in New Orleans."

23. Cohen, "New Orleans' Troubled Schools Get Overhaul."

24. People for the American Way, "Hurricane Katrina."

25. Linda Baker makes this important point about the embedded funding implications of "choice" in the context of how No Child Left Behind allows students to choose any school. Linda Baker, "All for One, None for All," *In These Times,* October 24, 2005, http://www.inthesetimes.com/site/main/article/2336/.

26. For an excellent discussion of the history of voucher debates, see Jeffrey Henig, *Rethinking School Choice* (Princeton, N.J.: Princeton University Press, 1994).

27. People for the American Way, "Hurricane Katrina."

28. See the eulogy for Walton, who died in a private airplane crash, in the right-wing Hoover Institution–published Fall 2005 issue of *Education Next* magazine, p. 5. It is important to mention that Walton's multibillion-dollar inheritance was the result of Wal-Mart's spectacular growth, which came from not only the entrepreneurial savvy of Sam Walton but also his commitment to union busting, displacing the cost of health care onto public coffers by refusing to offer adequate health insurance to employees, destroying small business throughout the United States through monopolistic practices, and, of course, being a significant contributor to the vast loss of manufacturing-sector work to China. See the excellent documentary film *Wal-Mart: The High Cost of Low Prices.*

29. Bolick, "Katrina's Displaced Students."
30. People for the American Way, "Hurricane Katrina."
31. The Editors, "Katrina's Lessons," *Rethinking Schools,* Fall 2005, 5.
32. Dial, "Emergency School Vouchers."
33. Dial, "Emergency School Vouchers."
34. People for the American Way, "Hurricane Katrina."
35. People for the American Way, "Hurricane Katrina."
36. *Heartland Institute School Reform News,* November 2005, 9, available at http://www.heartland.org.
37. Cohen, "New Orleans' Troubled Schools Get Overhaul."
38. George Wood, "Introduction," in *Many Children Left Behind,* ed. Deborah Meier and George Wood (Boston: Beacon, 2004), ix.
39. See U.S. Department of Education, *Volume I: Frequently Asked Questions, Emergency Impact Aid for Displaced Students,* January 12, 2006.
40. See U.S. Department of Education, *Volume I.*
41. Press Release, "Secretary Spellings Delivers Remarks on School Choice," April 5, 2006, www.ed.gov/news/pressreleases/2006/04/04052006.html.
42. Press Release, "Secretary Spellings Delivers Remarks on School Choice."
43. Judd Legum, Faiz Shakir, Nico Pitney, Amanda Terkel, Payson Schwin, and Christy Harvey, "Katrina: Ideology over People," ThinkProgress.Org, September 15, 2005, available at http://www.americanprogressaction.org.
44. Press Release, "Secretary Spellings, Gulf Coast Rebuilding Coordinator Powell Announce $1.1 Billion for Hurricane-Affected Students and Schools," March 2, 2006.
45. Monty Neil, "Leaving No Child Behind: Overhauling NCLB," in *Many Children Left Behind,* 102–3.
46. Mike Davis, "Who Is Killing New Orleans?" *The Nation,* April 10, 2006, http://www.thenation.com/doc/20060410/davis.
47. Adam Nossiter, "$29 Billion Package Buoys Hopes for Rebuilding Effort," *New York Times,* December 24, 2005, online edition.
48. Davis, "Who Is Killing New Orleans?" 14.
49. Davis, "Who Is Killing New Orleans?" 16.
50. Davis, "Who Is Killing New Orleans?" 16.

51. An exemplary case is the Metropolitan Planning Council, which brings together corporations and business professionals with housing and school experts and officials nationwide to foster such plans. For detailed and scholarly study of this process, see the work of Pauline Lipman, such as *High Stakes Education* (New York: Routledge, 2004). A number of liberal educational scholars, including Richard Kahlenberg and Richard Rothstein, fall prey to the logic of the urban cleansing trend by failing to situate school reform within the broader realities of neoliberal privatization and the dismantling of the public sector. Kahlenberg and Rothstein champion narrow school reform ideas such as the goal of expanding mixed-income schooling. While the urban cleansing schemes I am describing might achieve some modicum of this as an incidental effect, on the whole, such projects result in the creation of new or the expansion of already-existing economically and racially segregated enclaves. For example, the replacement of the Robert Taylor homes in Chicago has hardly resulted in broad-based economic integration in housing and schools or even the availability of high-quality housing and schooling. It has, however, resulted in residents moving to other poor neighborhoods to suffer the same kind of segregation that they were kicked out of. And it has also resulted in the spectacular enrichment of real estate developers and lawyers. Serious wide-scale economic and racial integration projects can be achieved by the public sector directly without such initiatives wasting billions of dollars by further enriching investors.

52. *Online NewsHour*, "Principals Challenges," November 9, 2005.

53. While corruption in the New Orleans public school system was a problem, not a single article I found discussed how chronic underfunding set within a web of broader conditions of poverty and social problems would inevitably inform administrative practices. One reason that the corruption at a business such as HealthSouth or Enron was so incomparably vaster than the public schools of New Orleans might have to do with the values institutionalized in each site. When profit becomes the prime motivator from which all other considerations follow, corruption is likely to be endemic. In my study of The Edison Schools, I found that the ceaseless push for high test scores to get investor capital resulted in pervasive testing corruption, misreporting of accounting and

numbers of school contracts, the use of paid public relations to create the appearance of popular support for the beleaguered company, and more.

54. http://www.sourcewatch.org.

55. D. J. Wilson, "Demolition Man," *Riverfront Times*, July 9, 2003.

56. Wilson, "Demolition Man."

57. *Online NewsHour*, "New Orleans Schools before and after Katrina," November 1, 2005, available at http://www.pbs.org.

58. Capochino, "More Than 100 N.O. Schools Still Closed."

59. See Saltman, *The Edison Schools*.

60. Kevin McCoy, "Alaska Firm Gets Gulf Rebuilding Job," *USA Today*, November 14, 2005.

61. The Editors, "Accountability at All Levels," *The Louisiana Weekly*, November 14, 2005.

62. Kevin McCoy, "Alaska Firm Gets Gulf Rebuilding Job," *USA Today*, November 14, 2005, http://www.usatoday.com/money/economy/employment/2005-09-29-katrina-contract-usat_x.htm.

63. Eric Lipton, "No-Bid Contract to Replace Schools after Katrina Is Faulted," *New York Times*, November 11, 2005, A1.

64. Lipton, "No-Bid Contract," A1.

65. Davis, "Who Is Killing New Orleans?" 12.

66. Gary Rivlin, "Anger Meets New Orleans Renewal Plan," *New York Times*, January 12, 2006, A18.

67. Rivlin, "Anger Meets New Orleans Renewal Plan," A18.

68. Davis, "Who Is Killing New Orleans?" 18.

69. Davis, "Who Is Killing New Orleans?" 18.

70. Cohen, "New Orleans' Troubled Schools Get Overhaul."

71. Davis, "Who Is Killing New Orleans?" 18.

72. "Crisis Drives Reinvention of New Orleans' Troubled Schools," *USA Today*, March 6, 2006, 12a.

73. Cohen, "New Orleans' Troubled Schools Get Overhaul."

74. Brian Riedlinger, quoted in *Charter Schools News Connection*, March 14, 2006, available at http://www.uscharterschools.org.

75. "Crisis Drives Reinvention," 12a.

76. "Crisis Drives Reinvention," 12a.

77. Rivlin, "New Orleans Commission to Seek Overhaul," A1.

78. *Online NewsHour*, "Rebuilding New Orleans Schools."

79. Cohen, "New Orleans' Troubled Schools Get Overhaul."

80. *Democracy Now!*, "New Orleans Residents and Evacuees Blast State of Schools, Housing, Jobs at Mayoral Forum," April 10, 2006, available at http://www.democracynow.org.

81. *Democracy Now!*, "New Orleans Residents and Evacuees."

82. See, for example, Cohen, "New Orleans' Troubled Schools Get Overhaul." Cohen participates in the bashing of the public schools while denying white supremacy, writing, "But for many New Orleans residents almost anything is better than the corruption-ridden, underperforming public school system that had long ago pushed middle-class, mostly white parents into paying for private education, deepening the city's racial divide." What is important here is the inversion of agency. Cohen mistakenly attributes the power and decision making over public school priorities to those with the least power and denies the systemic racism that drives white flight from schools.

83. Martin Carnoy, Rebecca Jacobsen, Lawrence Mishel, and Richard Rothstein, *The Charter School Dust-Up: Examining the Evidence on Enrollment and Achievement* (New York: Economic Policy Institute, Teachers College Press, 2005).

84. See, for example, Eric Rofes and Lisa Stulberg, eds., *The Emancipatory Promise of Charter Schools* (New York: State University of New York Press, 2004).

85. Amy Stuart Wells, *Where Charter School Policy Fails: The Problems of Accountability and Equity* (New York: Teachers College Press, 2002), 178.

86. Cohen, "New Orleans' Troubled Schools Get Overhaul."

87. John Pope, "Charter Schools Get Royal Treatment from Krewe," *The Times-Picayune*, February 27, 2006, online edition.

88. Pope, "Charter Schools Get Royal Treatment from Krewe."

89. For an excellent discussion of the political tendencies of the corporation, see Joel Bakan, *The Corporation* (New York: Free Press, 2004)—in particular, chap. 4, "Democracy, Ltd."

90. *Online NewsHour*, "Rebuilding New Orleans Schools."

91. Saltman, *The Edison Schools.*

92. It is important to note here that the Hoover Institution is a somewhat dubious source on the topic of The Edison Schools as it counts as a fellow John Chubb, who heads the company. At the American Educational Research Association annual meeting in 2006, Chubb served on a Hoover panel with Eric Hanuschek,

among others. I asked Chubb whether he thought there was "an accountability problem" with his claiming to be a neutral and objective educational researcher and yet getting paid by Edison. He replied that who pays him has nothing to do with his research and that his research "stands on its own."

93. Jessica L. Tonn, "New Orleans Charter Network Gets Underway," *Education Week,* January 18, 2006, 1–16.

94. Tonn, "New Orleans Charter Network Gets Underway," 1–16.

95. Tonn, "New Orleans Charter Network Gets Underway," 1–16.

96. Catherine Gewertz, "New Orleans Panel Rethinks School System," *Education Week,* January 11, 2006, 5–12.

97. Gewertz, "New Orleans Panel Rethinks School System."

98. Hill and Hannaway, "The Future of Public Education in New Orleans."

99. Saltman, *The Edison Schools.*

100. Hill and Hannaway, "The Future of Public Education in New Orleans," 12.

101. Steve Ritea, "La. Won't Run N.O. Schools by Itself," *The Times-Picayune,* January 3, 2006.

102. The Editors, "Katrina's Lessons."

2
Creative Associates International, Incorporated

Corporate Schooling and "Democracy Promotion" in Iraq

⌐⊖

Introduction

This chapter illustrates how global corporate educational initiatives, though profit motivated, sometimes function both as an instrument of foreign policy and as a manifestation of a broader imperial project.

According to neoconservative scholars as well as their critics, the events of September 11, 2001, allowed the implementation of premade plans to radically reshape the U.S. national security strategy to pursue more aggressively and openly global military and economic dominance and to force any and all nations to submit to a singular set of American values.[1] With the declaration of military response, the United States invaded first Afghanistan (2001) and then Iraq (2003), in part on the justification that these were fronts in the so-called war on terrorism.[2] Following both invasions, the United States, through the U.S. Agency for International Development (USAID), contracted with a private for-profit corporation, Creative Associates International, Incorporated (CAII), to lead the rebuilding of education. School buildings, textbooks, teacher preparation, curriculum planning, administration—all would be implemented by CAII directly or by firms subcontracted by CAII. In 2003, the company came under close scrutiny by Congress and the press for receiving its Iraq contracts without competitively bidding for them.[3] The no-bid contract with CAII was one of a number of no-bid contracts benefiting U.S. corporations, including Bechtel (which has been subcontracted by CAII to build schools), Halliburton, and others that profited from rebuilding in Iraq.[4]

What is at stake in the case of CAII in Iraq is not principally a matter of proper bidding protocol in educational contracting, or even merely the possibility that CAII was involved in "war profiteering,"[5] that the rebuilding "looks like a criminal racket,"[6] and that it is reaping "the windfalls of war."[7] The role of CAII in remaking education in Central Asia, the Middle East, and around the world on behalf of the United States concerns a number of broader issues about the international involvement of corporations in public education.

In one sense, CAII represents just one kind of international corporate involvement in schooling: educational development. Yet, the array of for-profit projects that CAII is involved with in Iraq, Afghanistan, and around the globe makes it exemplary of a range of global corporate schooling initiatives, including textbook production, curriculum design, remediation services, teacher education programs, and privatization schemes. As the first section of this chapter describes, CAII has been involved since the beginning of the "Reagan revolution" in "democracy promotion" projects that merged development work with political, military, and economic influence strategies on the part of the United States. I am concerned here with the changing relationship among nation-states, corporations, and education, as the United States under the Bush administration continues its neoconservative foreign policy that emphasizes the use of military force to install what its advocates describe as capitalist democracies modeled on the U.S. system.[8] Corporate education appears to have a central role in the neoconservative model as CAII appears on stage to rebuild following these military actions.

Writing of the Bush administration's Millennium Challenge Account (MCA), Susan Soederberg describes a neoconservative shift to what she calls "pre-emptive development," which could be extended to understand the use of CAII. Drawing on Panitch and Gindin, Soederberg explains the project of American imperialism to integrate the "non-integrating gap" into global capitalism through military force and also through a more concentrated development agenda that shifts the neoliberal Washington consensus loan conditionality strategies of the World Bank and IMF to a grant-withholding strategy typified by the MCA. If the strategy is different, the goal is the same: "that the path to increased growth and prosperity lies in countries' willingness and ability to adopt policies that promote economic freedom and the rule of bourgeois law (private property, the commodification and privatization of land, and so forth)."[9]

As Soederberg correctly identifies, the aim of integrating the "non-integrating gap" driving the neoliberal project contains constitutive problems and creates what she terms the security/insecurity paradox. Privatization, trade liberalization, and capital deregulation, the processes for the accumulation of capital (processes of profit-making, accumulation, and institutional regulation), produce certain kinds of security, while their concomitant erosion of the public sector and democratic control produces social and individual insecurity on all levels. "[T]he common sense assumption that unleashing the market will enhance economic prosperity of the majority not only has proven to be incorrect but also has led to a lack of popular support for neoliberal principles." The more overtly militarized neoconservative approach to U.S. foreign policy is in part a reaction to the crisis and failure of neoliberal global governance.[10]

There are a number of paradoxes in the way neoconservative ideology has been espoused and implemented. While the neoconservatives in rhetoric emphasize freedom, liberty, democracy, the rule of law, and free markets, they have championed domestic policies such as the USA Patriot

Act that severely restrict constitutional protections on privacy, rights, and legal representation, while simultaneously pursuing economic policies that aim to dismantle public spending on social programs, as well as wildly irresponsible fiscal budget and trade policy that has come under fire by the IMF and that uses state power to redistribute wealth to the richest citizens.

These economic policies have been described by many as crony capitalism for replacing market competition with sweetheart deals. At the same time, neoconservatives have roundly rejected the rules of international law to which the U.S. Constitution is bound, whether the matter is international criminal process, the environment, or the Geneva Conventions. Though there is much new about the present political constellation, CAII's history—for example, in support of the Contra guerillas in Nicaragua—highlights continuities in the role of education in aggressive U.S. foreign policy interventions in ways favorable to U.S.-based transnational capital. As the case of CAII illustrates, corporate educational development experts appear integral to U.S. economic and military strategy around the world. As the United States was developing a more sophisticated strategy to influence political process and educational apparatuses in the 1980s, CAII was there and has continued to be there, funded by USAID and working in conjunction with other corporations and nonprofit organizations.[11] In addition, CAII's 2003 takeover of educational development in Afghanistan signifies a break with the long-standing role that the public and nonprofit University of Nebraska played since the 1970s in making fundamentalist Islamic schools and texts to participate in creating the mujahideen that would serve the U.S. "market fundamentalist" project of driving out the Soviets. These mujahideen "good pupils" of Nebraskan texts would then become the nemesis of the United States in the form of the Taliban and Al Qaeda.

CAII's recent role in Iraq also signifies something new. If, as some have claimed, the Iraq war has been in part a radical free-market experiment bent on demolishing the public sector and shifting control of civil society nearly completely to the private sector, then education was not only a political and ideological concern of the United States, as in Afghanistan in the 1970s and 1980s. As Naomi Klein, Christian Parenti, Pratap Chatterjee, and others have argued, the Iraq war has been a radical experiment in wide-scale neoliberal privatization—an attempt to essentially hand a nation over to corporations.[12] They have also suggested that the military resistance to the United States in Iraq has been inextricably tied to attempts to retain control over industry and labor. Within this view education is, on the one hand, just another business opportunity provided for by war and, on the other hand, an experiment with the conservative U.S. domestic policy agenda of educational privatization that includes vouchers, charter schools, performance contracting, for-profit remediation, and the broad spectrum of educational reforms designed to set the stage for these privatization initiatives, including performance-based assessment, standardization of curriculum, and recourse to so-called scientific-based educational research.[13] But CAII, USAID, and the Department of Defense do not openly admit that their projects are foremost a matter of promoting a U.S. brand of capitalism. Rather, these projects are defined through "democracy promotion."

Such democracy promotion projects contain elements of neoliberal ideology in that they conflate economic values and political values while they ultimately exist to promote forms of political governance and modes of political subjectivity conducive to neoliberal economic policy. However, the neoconservative uses of democracy promotion projects differ from a Clinton-era type of neoliberal thought principally by emphasizing the use of coercion in the form of military power, whereas the Clintonians emphasized economic influence foremost.[14] Neoconservatism continues and intensifies the neoliberal model of diminishing the caregiving roles of the state while strengthening the repressive and punitive roles. This recourse to nationalism defines nationalism through consumerism, individualism, jingoistic patriotism, and with neoliberal terms such as Bush's "ownership society," which retains the ideal of the entrepreneurial subject and rejects values of social responsibility and civic participation. Yet, overseas democracy promotion projects have, since their inception, employed distinctly public-minded terms such as *civic education, civic participation, electoral reform,* and *democratic media reform.*

In what follows here, I will first recount the history of CAII and discuss its democracy promotion projects in Nicaragua, Haiti, and Iraq. I consider how these projects that claim to promote civic education, civic media, the expansion of individual rights, respect for constitutional rule and the rule of law, and the strengthening of the democratic process promote a version of democracy that is designed to be consistent with U.S. "interests." This is a version of democracy more representative of the power of an emergent transnational capitalist class than it is of the public in the nation in question. As William I. Robinson has argued, "In elaborating a policy of 'democracy promotion,' the United States is not acting on behalf of a 'U.S.' elite, but playing a leadership role on behalf of an emergent transnational elite."[15] This model of capitalist democracy requires political and economic reform consistent with the interests of capital in the richer nations. This includes privatization of state-controlled industry, deregulation of rules protecting domestic markets, and a number of civil society reforms consistent with these changes: (1) a depoliticized populace, (2) individualized consumer-oriented subjects who are decreasingly inclined to identify their interests with collective social action and increasingly inclined to identify their interests with consumption practices,[16] (3) a political subject friendly to heavy foreign involvement by powerful states and organizations, (4) reliance on expensive foreign-provided technology in the place of broad-based participatory civic involvement, (5) the reform of media and journalism on the private U.S. model, (6) the reform of political elections as intertwined with for-profit media on the U.S. model, and (7) an emphasis on privatization of state-run knowledge-making institutions.

In a theoretical sense, there is a question as to why the Bush administration, so bent on the pursuit of power through coercion, would also be so focused on producing hegemonic consent through the use of democracy promotion projects within nations targeted for military attack. Concern for education, public opinion, and knowledge-producing institutions like schools and mass media appears to remain high to an administration that has nonetheless shifted to a more overt use of force to achieve policy aims. On one level, the answer is that the Bush administration and the neoconservatives generally (quite unlike the Clintonians) understand the centrality of pedagogy to politics. They want to hand the environment over to polluting corporations or privatize Social Security or invade a nation, and they attempt to educate the public as to the virtue and necessity of doing so. This approach to governance is distinct from the long-standing approach of the Democratic party to build policy based on marketing feedback from voters rather than moral vision and political ideal. Granted, the moral visions and political ideals of the neoconservatives are more retrograde jingoism than principle and more often than not pretty propagandistic wrapping for corporate plunder. Nonetheless, the neocons selectively grasp the Gramscian insight that hegemony requires leadership, and political leadership demands educating those who are being led. Of course, the neocons have cared very little about making consent with the outer shell of foreign policy. As Giovanni Arrighi has written, hegemony is unraveling in the sense that the United States has lost its ability to lead other nations and is left with coercion.

To understand "democracy promotion" in relation to coercion and consent at a deeper level, it is instructive to employ the still-relevant distinction made by Louis Althusser, who was influenced by Antonio Gramsci—both of whom were influenced by and wrote about Machiavelli, a major figure of influence on the neoconservatives. Althusser viewed the state as an arm of capital yet emphasized Gramsci's recognition that the struggle for leadership of civil society is a crucial strategic, political, and pedagogical one, leading up to the revolutionary seizure of the bourgeois state (Ideological State Apparatuses, or ISAs, are both "stake and site" of struggle"). Althusser distinguished between the Repressive State Apparatus (RSA) (military, police, judicial system) and the Ideological State Apparatus (ISA) (schools, media, religions) to illustrate how the ruling capitalist class maintains control of the reproduction of the conditions of production through coercion and consent. He also emphasized that the RSA has crucial ideological components (the culture of the military matters decisively for repressive power to hold), while the ISAs contain crucial repressive elements (the disciplinary culture of the school keeps kids there to learn know-how in forms that are ideologically consistent with the ruling interests). Although there are numerous problems with many aspects of Althusser's thought, from the "scientism" to the class reductionism, to the failure to theorize sufficiently a theory of agency, to the many other problems accompanying the Marxist legacy, he nonetheless offers important tools for understanding the wielding of state power and the ways it has been increasingly used to undermine public democratic power in the United States and around the world.[17]

One crucial question that Althusser offers us now is what accounts for the shift in the wielding of state power from ISA to RSA—that is, from consent to coercion? To put it simply, why has there been a shift toward increasing use of overt repressive force on the part of the United States in foreign and domestic policy following an era of neoliberalism that emphasized the enforcement of the Washington Consensus principally through economic sanction and threats of economic and military force?[18] To complicate matters, why has U.S. civil society seen a rising culture of militarism that extends through popular culture and mass media and education? Perhaps most crucially, what to make of the concomitant rise in ISA activity internal to states targeted for "The New Imperialism"? In education, the United States is militarizing its own schools in numerous ways[19] while transforming Iraqi schools, at least in rhetoric, on the model of liberal and progressive education. As Althusser explained, RSAs have constitutive ideological components (e.g., the culture of the military) and ISAs have constitutive repressive dimensions (e.g., the compulsory attendance of schooling), yet why recent shifts?

David Harvey offers a compelling economic argument for the general shift to repression, explaining the shift from neoliberalism to neoconservatism: neoliberal policy was coming into dire crisis already in the late 1990s as deregulation of capital was resulting in a threat to the United States as it lost the manufacturing base and increasingly lost service-sector and financial industry to Asia. For Harvey, the new militarism in foreign policy is partly about a desperate attempt to seize control of the world's oil spigot as lone superpower parity is threatened by the rise of a fast-growing Asia and a unified Europe with a strong currency. Threats to the U.S. economy are posed by the potential loss of not only control over the fuel for the U.S. economy and military but also the power conferred by the dollar remaining the world currency, as the United States is increasingly indebted to China and Japan as they prop up the value of the dollar through the continued export of consumer goods. For Harvey, the structural problems behind global capitalism remain the Marxian crisis of overproduction driving down prices and wages while glutting the market and threatening profits and the financialization of the global economy. Capitalists and states representing capitalist interests respond to these crises through Harvey's version of what Marx called primitive accumulation, "accumulation by dispossession."

Put in the language of contemporary postmodern political theory, we might say that capitalism necessarily and always creates its own "other." The idea that some sort of "outside" is necessary for the stabilization of capitalism therefore has relevance. But capitalism can either make use of some pre-existing outside (non-capitalist social formations or some sector within capitalism—such as education—that has not yet been proletarianized) or it can actively manufacture it.... The "organic relation" between expanded reproduction on the one hand and the often violent processes of dispossession on the other has shaped the historical geography of capitalism. This helps us better understand what the capitalist form of imperialism is about.[20]

As Harvey explains, privatization is one of the most powerful tools of accumulation by dispossession, transforming publicly owned and controlled goods and services like education into private and restricted ones—the continuation of "enclosing the commons" begun in Tudor England. Though CAII's democracy promotion projects around the world often have an appearance of progressive encouragement of civic participation, individual rights, and constitutional rule of law, they primarily exist to encourage capitalist democracy modeled on the privatized and privatizing U.S. system. These programs tend to target nations with a strong socialist tradition that understands welfare state programs, state-owned industry, and strong labor unions as natural and beneficial to society. Democracy promotion programs tend to emphasize individual freedoms and rights while favoring the dismantling of projects and institutions that provide individuals with collective security. Thus, while appearing to promote rights and justice, the underlying political and cultural strategy should be seen as promoting not so much participatory democratic culture but rather what Zygmunt Bauman refers to as the "Individualized Society" that benefits capital interests in the United States and the economic elite in the nation in question.

If privatization is a major aim of democracy promotion programs, then making the right kind of individual subjects for the privatized economy and state is a second major aim. The content of democracy promotion projects aims at making privatized subjects more intent on individual consumption than on democratic citizens capable of genuine self-governance. That is, these programs discourage skills, dispositions, identifications, values, and ideals conducive to the widespread democratic control over politics, economy, and culture. At the same time that these programs encourage privatization and consumerism, they also encourage an authoritarianism that is best understood by the expanding authoritarian culture found in the United States.[21] As Harvey explains, if neoliberalism came into crisis due to the excesses of capitalism (deregulation and liberalization yielding capital flight, deindustrialization, etc.), then the neocon response emphasizing control and order and reinvigorated overt state power makes a lot of sense.[22]

As I discussed in the introduction, there is a crucial tension presently between two fundamental functions of public education for the capitalist state. On the one hand, public education aims to reproduce the conditions of production: teaching skills and know-how in ways that are ideologically compatible with the social relations of capital accumulation. Public education, whether in the United States or Iraq, makes political and economic leaders or docile workers and marginalized citizens, or even participates in sorting and sifting out those to be excluded from economy and politics completely. On the other hand, the relatively new and growing function involves the capitalist possibilities of pillaging public education for profit. Rather than addressing the funding inequalities and the intertwined dynamics at work in making poor schools, the remedy is commodification. Such a "smash and grab" approach to ideological state apparatuses appears in Iraq, as we will see, as infrastructure is devastated through sanction and war and followed up with privatization and decentralization.

The operations of CAII raise a number of crucial questions about the role of the corporation in U.S. foreign policy: How are democratic commitments being defined and enacted in foreign education and media aid? To what extent is educational development an investment in a potentially inexpensive labor force for U.S.-based capital and the formation of a consumer base for U.S. corporations under the guise of national security? To what extent is the project of corporate globalization being implemented through military action while being redefined through the discourses of personal safety and democratic ideals? The overarching and related question I raise through the example of CAII is whether such democracy promotion projects are best understood as fostering or hindering the expansion of democratic social relations in the areas of politics, economy, and culture. I conclude by suggesting that progressive educators ought to link global corporate schooling initiatives with broad geopolitical questions, cultural politics, and pedagogical approaches that offer new modes of interpretation that can become acts of intervention. The first section offers a brief overview of the history of CAII and then details CAII's operations in Nicaragua and Haiti. The second section focuses on Iraq.

Creative Associates International, Incorporated

Creative Associates International, Incorporated, was founded in 1979 by four women who had been partners in a day care business. Maria Charito Kruvant, Ilda Cheryl Jones, Diane Trister Dodge, and Mimi Tse began the company in Kruvant's basement as a for-profit management consulting company through the Small Business Administration's minority-owned business program. Creative Associates got its first contract with USAID to "help poor women" in Kruvant's native Bolivia and brought in less than $100,000 in its first year.[23] When in 1983 Jones left the firm, the partners changed the name to Creative Associates International, Inc. By 1985, CAII was a multimillion-dollar business with government and business contracts. It has received more than four hundred contracts around the world with offices in eleven countries, more than three hundred employees, and annual revenue as high as $50 million.[24] It works or has worked in Angola, El Salvador, Haiti, Afghanistan, Jordan, Benin, Guatemala, Lebanon, Liberia, Mozambique, Nicaragua, South Africa, Peru, Serbia, and Montenegro. Ninety percent of its revenue comes from USAID, while clients include the U.S. Marine Corps and the World Bank.

According to the *Washington Times,* Kruvant and her cofounders started the company to move from the nonprofit sector into the business world and make "at least a little money doing development work."[25] Kruvant and CAII have made quite a bit more than "a little money" from CAII's contracts in Iraq alone.

> As was the case last school year, the U.S. government's support for education reconstruction in Iraq is provided primarily through a USAID contract with Creative Associates. That contract, which *Education Week* received through a Freedom of Information Act request, estimates payment of $56.5 million to the firm for two years of work, with an additional payment of $52 million also possible for that time period. The firm also stands to earn $82.6 million more from the USAID if the contract is extended beyond two years.[26]

Kruvant has come to own 69 percent of CAII, with Mimi Tse owning the other 31 percent.

Born in La Paz, Kruvant is the daughter of a wealthy landowning family forced to flee to Argentina in 1955. In 1963, Kruvant studied in New Jersey, went to Argentina to earn a teaching degree, and then returned to New Jersey to work with "disadvantaged children."[27] "She was involved in passing federal legislation to promote bilingual education, founded centers for bilingual education in several states, and helped develop bilingual education programs in the Washington, D.C., area and New York."[28] Kruvant's early inclination for liberal if not progressive educational perspectives appears on the surface to extend to CAII's contemporary work. Robert Gordon, CAII's director of operations, described the company's work in Iraq as involving not just assessing what needs to be done with the education system, rebuilding schools, redesigning curriculum, and developing teacher training but also, as Gordon stated, "We want them to get away from rote learning. We want students to be able to ask questions."[29]

The popular press has seized on CAII's educational development work in Iraq and the fact that it is a minority-owned business as the ultimate argument against progressive and left-wing criticisms of the Iraq war as an imperial oil war waged for the strategic and economic benefit of the United States.[30] *The Economist,* which admits that the war profiteering is much broader than oil, nonetheless relies on CAII to suggest that the profiteering is hardly driven by cronyism. In a section called "Phony Cronyism," the magazine wrote a month after the U.S. invasion:

> In truth, the bidders are a broad church.... Charito Kruvant, president of Creative Associates International, a "minority, women-owned and managed firm," based in Washington, DC, that is said to be USAID's preferred choice to revamp Iraq's education system, does not sound like a typical conservative crony of Mr. Cheney. She signs the firm's "message from our president" with "Peace, Charito."[31]

If CAII is used in the popular press as evidence that the war was not driven by crony capitalism, it is also used to highlight the ethnic diversity and inclusiveness of the corporate economy. The magazine *Hispanic Business* acclaims CAII as a minority success story, ranking it number 113 on the "Hispanic Business 500."

> Businesses grow when they supply a need. At Creative Associates International, the need sounds abstractly idealistic—the creation of free and orderly societies. But as a service firm helping countries develop democratic institutions and improve education systems, Creative Associates has what the current federal procurement market demands. Steve Horblitt, vice-president for external relations, says.... "We work mostly in

countries that have gone through a major change recently." . . .
"But we don't export anything—we transfer ideas and know-
how." Providing that service garnered Creative Associates
revenues of $39.3 million in 2002, up from $26 million the
previous year.[32]

Idealism, peace, critical thinking, multiculturalism.
What, then, is CAII? A group of well-meaning progressive
educators who have discovered how to have their efforts in
war-torn regions be well remunerated? Are Kruvant, Tse,
Gordon, Horblitt, and company a cohort of idealists merely
responding to political events to further their goals and
ideals under the umbrage of the United States' pursuit of its
strategic interests and national security strategy? Or is CAII
and global U.S.-based corporate educational development
contracting a constitutive element of a long-standing U.S.
imperial[33] project?

To begin answering these questions, it is necessary to
examine who CAII has worked with in the past, what other
organizations CAII is involved with, and how CAII's activities
fit into the broader educational dimension of U.S. national
security strategy.

The representation of Kruvant in mass media as principally a symbol of the successes of minority-owned business,
as an innocent idealist, maybe even as a hippie holdover
who disproves crony capitalism could not be farther from
the intersection of multimillion-dollar profits and foreign
intervention planning work that characterizes Kruvant's
enterprise. Kruvant is involved in government policy and
Washington, D.C., business circles, having worked on the
Project in Search of a National Security Strategy.

Kruvant has served as chair of the advisory board of the U.S.
Small Business Administration's Washington District Office. She
has held the Small Business Administration's Advisory Council
public meetings at Creative's headquarters. She has also been
President of the board of directors of the Society for International Development's Washington chapter, and member of the

Economic Club of Washington, D.C. . . . and served as president
of the National Association of Women Business Owners' D.C.
chapter.[34]

Kruvant sits on the boards of Venture Philanthropy Partners,
Calvert Group, and Acacia Federal Savings Bank, described
by John M. Derrick Jr., chairman and CEO of Pepco, as "a
visible and respected member of the D.C. business community."[35] As such, Kruvant worked to find financial opportunities for large corporations by introducing them to D.C. small
businesses. "From 1996 until 2000, Kruvant served as an
emergency schools trustee after the D.C. financial control
board stripped the elected board of its powers."[36] These
domestic activities of seizing an educational system and
representing business interests as democratic governance
and philanthropy share a marked resemblance to CAII's
international work, as the remainder of this chapter will
elaborate.

CAII in Nicaragua and Haiti

In 1989, Congress and the first Bush administration officially
stopped military aid to the Contra guerrillas in Nicaragua
who had been fighting the Sandinista government. After
more than a century of direct and indirect military attack
on Nicaragua that included a quarter-century span of twelve
U.S. military invasions, the United States last invaded directly
in 1933. It was in this year that the United States left behind
the National Guard under control of Anastasio Somoza, who
would establish a family dynasty. Throughout the Somozas'
reign, the National Guardsmen, "consistently maintained
by the United States, passed their time on martial law, rape,
torture, murder of the opposition, and massacres of peasants,
as well as less violent pursuits such as robbery, extortion,
contraband, running brothels and other government functions. . . . The Somoza clan laid claim to the lion's share of
Nicaragua's land and business."[37] Somoza's rule secured U.S.

capital in Nicaragua, such as the United Fruit Company. By 1979, when the last Somoza was overthrown by the Sandinistas, he left a nation in which two-thirds of the population earned $300 per year. Somoza arrived for a comfortable exile in the United States, having drained nearly a billion dollars from his country. Following the Carter administration's attempt to undermine the Sandinistas with the Central Intelligence Agency (CIA), Ronald Reagan's election resulted in open support for the reestablished National Guard in the form of the Contra "freedom fighters." As the United States waged economic war on Nicaragua, the U.S.-armed and -funded Contras committed egregious acts of terrorism against civilians.

> The contras' brutality earned them a wide notoriety. They regularly destroyed health centers, schools, agricultural cooperatives, and community centers—symbols of the Sandinistas' social programs in rural areas. People caught in these assaults were often tortured and killed in the most gruesome ways.... "Rosa had her breasts cut off. Then they cut into her chest and took out her heart. The men had their arms broken, their testicles cut off, and their eyes poked out. They were killed by slitting their throats and pulling the tongue out through the slit."[38]

The United States funded, armed, directed, and participated in these activities. It also funded through the CIA and Oliver's North's secret operations Cardinal Miguel Obando and the Catholic Church of Nicaragua, which put part of the hundreds of thousands of U.S. dollars toward "religious instruction" to "thwart the Marxist-Leninist policies of the Sandinistas."[39]

Enter CAII in 1989 when the United States was pouring money into Nicaragua toward defeating the Sandinistas in the 1990 election. The United States through the "National Endowment for Democracy [NED] spent more than 11 million dollars, directly or indirectly on the election campaign in Nicaragua."[40] Election laws were circumvented by building up the National Opposition Union (UNO) with millions of dollars run through NED for "nonpartisan" and "prodemocracy" programs, voter education, voter registration, and job skill programs. (Of course, such foreign meddling in domestic elections is illegal in the United States.) The United States only funded the UNO out of eight political parties. At this time Creative Associates was contracted by the U.S. Defense Department to "help persuade the Contras to lay down their arms," and CAII helped to integrate the Contras into Nicaraguan civil society. The United States continued to fund the Contras, who campaigned for the UNO in rural places. According to the Center for Public Integrity,

> Kruvant reportedly helped to convince the Contras that the Nicaraguan government wouldn't execute them if they surrendered. In 1989, as part of a $27 million USAID package, Creative received $1 million to train Contra rebels in skills such as road maintenance, first aid and engine repair. As part of the project, known as "Training in Delivery Systems," Creative coordinated 29 vocational courses to teach more than 600 Contras. In an April 1990 election, the Sandinistas were voted out of power and replaced by the National Opposition Union.[41]

CAII's activities in Nicaragua constituted part of a new democracy promotion program that began with the formation of the NED and that shifted prior activities of the CIA to more sophisticated operations by USAID, NED, and other public and private organizations.[42] William I. Robinson, who explains that the model in Nicaragua was the testing ground for the current Iraq strategy, aptly describes how democracy promotion programs are tiered with multiple levels of policy design, funding, operational activity, and influence. At the top the White House, Pentagon, CIA, State Department, and other branches target regions and nations for intervention synchronized with broader foreign policy objectives as well as military, economic, and other dimensions. For Robinson, the second tier is composed of USAID, which in turn distributes hundreds of millions of dollars directly or through the

NED or other agencies, such as the US Institute for Peace (USIP) and Creative Associates International.[43]

"Democratship" in Haiti

Shortly after its work in Nicaragua, CAII was involved with the 1991 coup against democratically elected president Jean-Bertrand Aristide, which was led by Lieutenant General Raoul Cedras and Colonel Michel François. Haiti, which had suffered for decades under the brutal regimes of U.S.-supported "Papa Doc" Duvalier and then his son "Baby Doc" Duvalier, remained the poorest nation in the hemisphere.[44] When Duvalier escaped a popular uprising in Haiti in 1986, a series of unpopular governments finally resulted in the landslide election of Aristide, a Catholic priest with a background in liberation theology. Within eight months, Cedras and François staged the coup that resulted in the killing of four thousand Haitians by the regime, an exodus of "boat people," and a trade embargo against the military regime by the United States and the Organization of American States (OAS).

> Cedras and François responded with a smear campaign against Aristide. After expelling him from the country, they rummaged through Aristide's diaries and personal effects in search of incriminating evidence. Predictably, this "investigation" concluded that Aristide was a "psychotic manic-depressive with homicidal and necrophiliac tendencies." The junta transmitted these charges to the US news media through an array of hired lobbyists and PR representatives, including George Demougeot, who also represented a US apparel firm with an assembly plant in Haiti, and Stephen A. Horblitt and Walter E. Faunteroy of Creative Associates International Inc.[45]

CAII's work in assisting the coup leaders against the democratically elected leader appears to starkly contrast with the corporation's overt mission of democracy promotion. It is also curious considering that the United States' official position against the military regime was seemingly contradictory with funding CAII as it attempted to discredit President Aristide. Stephen A. Horblitt's writing about democracy and Haiti perhaps clarifies this contradiction. In a 1996 CSIS "working paper" titled "The State of Leadership: Haiti," Horblitt explains the need for a form of government that he calls "democratship" that merges democratic governance with dictatorship in executing decisions. Horblitt's version of politics describes democratship as a "management concept" and continues to explain that its development would need to be supported externally. Calling for leadership in Haiti that is consistent with neoliberal "Washington consensus" economic policy, Horblitt identifies the problem with Haiti's political system as hindering free-market competition. "The task for Haitian leadership is to end the practice of government by franchise and domination of the market by monopolies, private or state-owned."[46] Writing nothing of his own involvement in Haitian politics, his support for dictators, and undermining of democratic elections five years earlier, Horblitt immediately continues, "If dictatorship is to end, politics must be secondary to a market economy."[47] This is a startling statement. Market economies have historically been quite compatible with dictatorships. From Nazi Germany to Pinochet's Chile, there are numerous examples to suggest that dictatorship and market economies are hardly mutually exclusive. Such a succinct statement of neoliberal policy that views politics as economics helps clarify the extent to which what is termed "democracy promotion" may be more consistent with redefining politics through the support of political groups and parties that favor U.S. support of transnational capital while aiming to redefine politics itself as best understood through economics.

Diversity, Horblitt goes on to say, is central to this vision of "democratship." What does diversity mean for Horblitt?

This means that the identification and support of leadership will have to be diverse. Diverse leadership does exist in several sectors that define Haiti. There are leaders in private business, labor, nongovernmental organizations (NGOs), religious groups, women's organizations, and civil and human rights organizations, in addition to political parties and the government. New leadership also must come from the newly-created Haitian police force.[48]

In Horblitt's view, pluralism and diversity foster an environment favorable to privatization and liberalization of trade, an environment good for doing business, and an environment that views government as corrupt and corrupted without addressing how the legacy of colonialism and his very own actions participated in the abuse of state actions. This is to say nothing of describing as diversity the involvement in political leadership by the new police force—a police force that would go on to commit systematic murder of political opponents supporting President Aristide and his party Lavalas following the kidnapping/coup against him in 2004.[49] Horblitt's version of democracy is hardly original. As William I. Robinson explains, this pluralistic model of "democracy promotion" has a trajectory quite different from popular democracy.

> What U.S. policymakers mean by "democracy promotion" is the promotion of *polyarchy*. Polyarchy refers to a system in which a small group actually rules and mass participation in decision-making is confined to leadership choice in elections carefully managed by competing elites. The pluralist assumption is that elites will respond to the general interests of majorities, through polyarchy's "twin dimensions" of "political contestation" and "political inclusiveness," as a result of the need of those who govern to win a majority of votes. The polyarchic definition of democracy was developed in U.S. academic circles closely tied to the policymaking community in the United States in the post–World War II years.[50]

Robinson's statements emphasize that the meaning of democracy is highly contested and that the contest over claiming and defining the term cannot be separated from

Chapter 2

material and symbolic power struggles. As such, claims to the meaning of democracy not only in U.S. policy circles but in Haitian, Nicaraguan, or Iraqi media and in classrooms have tremendous implications for who is to rule and how. In the case of CAII, it is important to recognize that what passes as democracy promotion includes the support for polyarchy through the institution of U.S.-style money-driven elections and constitutional rule oriented toward protecting property interests foremost. CAII's work on media reform and educational rebuilding does emphasize particular versions of civic participation and constitutional rule of law. However, it does not emphasize or include or promote forms of popular democracy that would involve the public in deliberating or debating or controlling the future of national material resources or symbolic and cultural values. CAII's RAMAK project in Haiti exemplifies this distinction between the promotion of polyarchy and the promotion of participatory forms of democratic governance.

From 2001 to the 2004 coup/kidnapping of Aristide by the United States, CAII worked to influence the Haitian media and justice systems with a focus on expanding radio journalism toward a private, for-profit media and teaching journalists how to cover elections in ways closer to the U.S. media system, including the professional code of reporting that includes the guise of disinterested objectivity. This proposes a shift away from the partisan press that allows viewers and listeners to understand clearly the relationship between party/ideological allegiance and the operative assumptions guiding reporting. The guise of objectivity conceals the inevitably political nature of journalism and other media content. The goal of depoliticizing the partisan Haitian media and civil society generally should be understood as a strategy to narrow the range of political debate and values to frame out particularly left-wing perspectives that would stand to put public interests over capital interests. CAII's 2002–2003 report explains their objectives in Haiti:

90

During the second year of the Haiti Media Assistance and Civic Education Project, Creative Associates (known by its Creole acronym, RAMAK) continued to implement activities in support of two complementary objectives: increasing citizen awareness and everyday application of rights and responsibilities; and strengthening journalists' ability to report on issues related to democratic development and to advocate for greater freedom of the press.[51]

While it is difficult to gauge the value of CAII's RAMAK project or how it is received by the Haitian public, it appears to encourage privatization of community-based radio, to proselytize aspects of U.S.-style formal democracy, and to rely heavily on the promise of expensive equipment to entice stations and listeners to warm to the content and organizational demands of CAII, with a heavy emphasis on commercial media concerns such as fund-raising. "RAMAK plans to host a community radio conference in January 2004.... The three-day conference will include plenary sessions on the philosophy of community radios, specialized workshops on management, fundraising, marketing, programming, basic skills, feature stories on local heroes, good news stories, and civic education themes, among others."[52] The heavy emphasis on fund-raising appears in CAII's literature to be just as much about training in running money-driven elections as it does about teaching station workers the virtues of an entrepreneurial form of community radio that will guarantee that those who can give the most will get the most. To consider the political implications of such programs, it is helpful to consider democratic media at the very least in terms of production and consumption.[53]

Democratic media production would expand access to media production to the widest array of citizens and political viewpoints while protecting against both state and corporate media monopolies. As Robert McChesney has argued, democratizing media in the United States would require redistributing the excessive production control that corporations currently have over media so that a greater range of people, perspectives, and ideological views could enter into public deliberation in this public sphere as media producers. Strong support for public media would need to be coupled with demonopolization to ensure expansive access to media production. In addition, democratic media requires democratization of media consumption. As mass communications scholars and proponents of critical media literacy, critical pedagogy, and cultural studies have argued, citizens can learn practices of media interpretation that can link crucial public questions and problems to the pedagogical and political roles that media plays. These traditions of thought suggest that media teaches not just information and facts but also values, ideologies, and identifications, from which individuals draw frameworks of interpretation, commonsense understandings, and assumptions about the world. Critical media literacy teaches tools of interpretation that can foster practices of democratic intervention and participation.

RAMAK goes in the opposite direction of these democratic media approaches by working to commercialize and privatize media production while linking successful production to the use of more expensive foreign equipment. RAMAK aims to "professionalize" radio by shifting production controls over finance and management and fund-raising to specialists with modes of operating patterned on U.S. models of corporate management. As the United States was blocking crucial financial aid before the ouster, RAMAK appeared to encourage Haitian media not only to rely on more expensive equipment but to follow the U.S. commercial media model, with emphasis on an abundance of content devoid of meaningful debate and discussion, hollowed out of ideological controversy, and without policy debate that links contemporary news to broader historical realities and power struggles. As a forum for such debate and deliberation, radio stands as a potential element of the public sphere that can provide information for informed democratic participation as well as tools of interpretation that can foster acts of political participation. While civic education programming would ideally encourage this, little evidence indicates that RAMAK does so. As CAII's report continues, this becomes quite evident.

> RAMAK staff also brought balance to an explosive situation in the Grande Anse area, where four different stations were serving different political and philosophical tendencies. Partisans of the stations fought each other, resulting in the death of one person. RAMAK decided to help upgrade equipment in all the stations—Radyo Rebelle, Radyo Dame Marie, Radyo Zantray and Radyo Pipirit—to avoid choosing sides. Through the process, tensions between the stations were eased and these stations now acknowledge publicly that the upgrade in equipment is the "fruit of reconciliation."[54]

Rather than providing a mechanism for open and engaged debate on these different political and philosophical tendencies, apparently CAII views provision of expensive equipment funded by the United States to be a more democratic alternative. Buying off competing ideological parties with bribes replaces political engagement in this model. The program supports media production that shifts control to those who invest in and control expensive equipment. Such control guarantees that the class interests of the media are more aligned with those of transnational capital and less aligned with Haiti's poor, which constitute the vast majority of the population.

A central dimension of RAMAK content is a soap opera series that heavily emphasizes law-and-order themes teaching submission of citizens to authority rather than preparedness for participating in wielding authority in multiple aspects of civil society. CAII reports, "The impact of the civic education soap opera series—which through story-telling deals with a range of issues including corruption, justice, and solidarity—was undeniable at the conference."[55] There is quite a difference in "civic education" that stresses obedience to authority and civic education that promotes civic participation. Likewise, closer examination of what passes as civic education in the soap opera series belies a rejection of the political and partisan nature of the press. RAMAK appears simultaneously to denounce the Haitian justice system under Aristide while also suggesting that the values and control over civil society are not thoroughly political. CAII's report justifies content of the soap opera:

> Today, civil society sometimes replaces the state or the government, inefficient in a lot of areas. Civil society can help by: • Questioning, by discussing the problems • Facilitating the introduction of civic actions • Helping bring the problem(s) at a higher level than the individual • Serving as a model, a reference for action. But for actions to have greater impact and to carry the message further, it is necessary to have alliances between civil society and citizens. However, when civic society becomes "political" it becomes inefficient.[56]

What is wrong with this is that first CAII denounces state authority as inevitably corrupt, and then it denies the political nature of civil society. The denial of the political nature of civil society is part of a neoliberal agenda that aims to make business values the apparent natural and neutral fabric of civil society. Such values are hardly politically neutral. CAII employs the language of civil society, civic participation, and solidarity while denouncing the political struggles that are waged through and over civil society. Thus, the meaning of civil society for CAII can only be understood as a redescription of the public sector in terms that describe the private sector as they promote individualistic consumerism at the expense of public and political solidarity while representing the interests of business as universal values. Solidarity, voided of its political and ideological dimensions, then becomes a call for consensus to the rules of the game, with a denied access to shape the rules. If democracies are constituted by public struggles over values, meanings, resources, and institutions, then they require mechanisms in civil society for such struggles to be waged. By denying politics and fostering privatization programs such as RAMAK, CAII diminishes the capacity of educative institutions to be a public sphere where such genuine civic engagement is possible. Of course, CAII's way of "promoting democracy," though it may not foster genuine democratic politics through engaged political debate and deliberation, does forge allegiances to the sponsor of the gifts and unite dissenting views under the umbrage of USAID money. The emphasis on shifting media control away from the state and toward a private for-profit system stands to encourage a reliance on foreign-provided expensive equipment and a depoliticized media system in which the market and concerns with profit largely become the "neutral" fabric of the new media. Considering that CAII's project was intertwining media and election transformations, such political influence could stand to be quite useful when Washington found a need to replace the government of Haiti.

What is more, if aspects of RAMAK did promote civic participation, such encouragement needs to be understood in terms of the broader strategic aims of those funding it. More specifically, it is quite clear that the policy goals behind building a grassroots movement against Aristide through RAMAK and other programs are consistent with the planning for President Aristide's removal from office in 2004, the installation of a ruling group more pleasing to Washington, and the killing and purging from government of Aristide supporters. The new interim Haitian government was stacked with those tied to international organizations committed to the United Nations (UN) and its Bretton Woods Institutions that have "been very active in Haiti for many decades without making any discernible progress with the country's social or economic development."[57] The interim minister of commerce following the 2004 coup, Danielle St. Lot, was, since August 2003, director of training for RAMAK.

Despite a near-total absence of U.S. media coverage of Haiti after the 2004 coup, there is little evidence yet of the broad-based and inclusive democratic participation in the new Haitian government celebrated in the writing of Horblitt or of RAMAK. Nor has there been much progress on the free-market competition that Horblitt called for in his writing. On the contrary, the new government has acted to secure the interests of the transnational elite of rich citizens rather than the roughly 85 percent of the destitute Haitian population that continued to support Aristide.[58] This is hardly surprising considering that in 2002, the Brookings Institution hosted the first meeting of the Haiti Democracy Project, which included the U.S. ambassador to OAS, Roger Noriega, former head of USAID, and CAII executives and representatives of the Haitian expatriate and business elite. This group went on to organize protests against Aristide in Washington prior to the coup/kidnapping. Statements by participants at the meeting made the agenda clear. Assistant Secretary-General of OAS Luigi Einaudi "opened the talks with dire predictions that Haiti was fast approaching a point where diplomatic means would no longer contribute to solve the crisis."[59] The *Miami Herald* quoted James Morell, the executive director of the Haiti Democracy Project: "The dilemma facing policymakers is to determine the 'way to stability.' ... 'Something has really changed in Haiti. The divine mandate is over.'"[60] The *Herald* continued by quoting the same Stephen Horblitt, a consultant with Creative Associates International:

> "The prospects simply aren't good," said Steve Horblitt, a political scientist and longtime analyst of U.S.-Haiti relations. "The government of Haiti continues its long history of not being a provider of services but an extractor. What happens in Haiti affects the United States." ... "This administration needs to have a real clear reexamination of policy. The U.S. can help Haiti, but it can't help without a partner there. We need to be very clear about our interests and our principles and we need to make it clear to that gentleman [Aristide] that we're not playing."[61]

Horblitt's remarkable statements would seem to make more sense by replacing "the government of Haiti" with "the government of the United States": the government of the United States continues its long history of being not a provider of services but an extractor, and what happens in the United States affects Haiti.

The same *Herald* article selectively explains the crisis facing Haiti and the ways the Haitian government was acting against U.S. interests and principles, including cooperatives in farming, fishing, and housing that would potentially cost investors financial losses, a fuel shortage, and international aid money being withheld on the basis that the opposition party contested the number of seats it should have in the parliament. What the article does not say is what role the United States played in the allegations made against the cooperatives that resulted in financial trouble, or the role in stopping international financial assistance, or the relationship between the United States and the opposition party, or about how any of this may have fueled popular discontent with the frustrated Haitian public, the vast majority of whom continued to support Aristide before and after the 2004 coup. More important, the article does not say what Paul Farmer, an American physician working in Haiti for twenty years, said six months after the 2004 coup:

> There has been no visible improvement from the vantage point of the rural poor. The real crises in Haiti are humanitarian and political. ... The humanitarian crisis will only be addressed by dealing with hunger, excess burden of disease, unsafe drinking water and dangerous roads. These were the problems that were to be addressed by the aid that was blocked by the U.S. administration for the three years preceding Aristide's removal. ... It's popular to say things like "The Haitians have to solve their own problems," but it's silly. The Haitians did not create slavery, chronic interference with their internal affairs, gunboat diplomacy, foreign occupations and a long history of trade and aid embargoes. The Haitians did not create unfair economic

policies. These were created outside of Haiti. Erasing Haiti's debt, restoring constitutional rule, ending arbitrary aid embargoes and sinking significant resources into public health, public education and public infrastructure would be central to addressing and indeed solving Haiti's social problems.[62]

Despite the rhetoric of democracy and civic participation, Creative Associates International's work in Haiti did not help the public address this historical legacy. However, it does seem to be the case that privatization of public infrastructure is clearly on the agenda of USAID and CAII but is also facilitated in part by the World Bank. As Naomi Klein writes, following the ouster of Aristide,

> in exchange for a $61 million loan, the bank is requiring "public-private partnership and governance in the education and health sectors," according to bank documents—i.e. private companies running schools and hospitals. Roger Noriega, US Assistant Secretary of State for Western Hemisphere Affairs, has made it clear that the Bush Administration shares these goals. "We will also encourage the government of Haiti to move forward, at the appropriate time, with restructuring and privatization of some public sector enterprises," he told the American Enterprise Institute on April 14, 2004.[63]

Klein aptly titles this process "disaster capitalism," which recalls Harvey's "accumulation by dispossession." The tension between dispossession and reproduction that is central to imperialism for Harvey needs to be understood internationally and intranationally. So the reproduction function that Haiti serves global capital (cheap labor potential for manufacturing and agriculture) relates to plans for the education sector (USAID does basic education projects, or BEPs). Democratic education and democratic media—should they expand public control over politics, culture, and economy—may threaten the reproduction of social relations conducive to the capital accumulation of a transnational class. CAII undermines democratic education and democratic media by fostering concentrated control through privatization while calling the initiatives democratic.

In short, despite CAII's important role in executing U.S. strategies for replacing the democratically elected government of Haiti, there is little evidence of democracy having been promoted. Only with the history of CAII's work in civil society on elections, conflict reconciliation, and media reform prior to their Iraq contracts can the company's role in education rebuilding be understood.

CAII in Iraq

CAII's operations in Iraq have been mostly covered in the press in terms of corruption scandal over no-bid contracting and efficient delivery of educational services. Almost nowhere has press coverage addressed the privatization agenda of educational restructuring in Iraq or the political implications that privatization of education has for the nation. If privatization is a continuity in the neoconservative agenda from neoliberalism, then corruption and cronyism appear as a discontinuity with the neoliberal ideals of competition. Yet neoliberalism, while focused on competition and efficiency in rhetoric, was principally focused on using this rhetoric to dictate the terms for economically weak entities. Accumulation by dispossession or primitive accumulation, as Harvey reminds us, is described by Marx as a return to theft. This allows us to see how corruption and privatization go hand in hand as a strategy of empire. In what follows, I discuss the coverage of corruption and efficient delivery of educational services as well as claims that CAII is involved in implementing "democratic education" in Iraq. I conclude by suggesting that this coverage has obscured the conservative educational privatization agenda, which is possibly the most radical aspect of educational rebuilding and which straddles accumulation by dispossession and accumulation by reproduction.

In March 2004, a year after the United States invaded Iraq, the Departments of Defense and State released optimistic reports on the situation in Iraq, whereas the Brookings Institution[64] painted a different picture of reconstruction and security in its "Iraq Index," finding that only 65 percent of local security forces are fully trained, that only 2 percent of the 8,500 "anti-coalition suspects" held in detention were foreign nationals despite the claim by State and Defense that the insurgency is composed mostly of "foreign terrorists," that monthly electricity levels were less than prewar levels, and that only two-thirds of the population had access to potable water.[65] Reporting on these conflicting versions of the state of Iraq, the *Atlantic Monthly* wrote, "Perhaps the brightest spot is education: more than 2,300 schools have been rehabilitated by USAID, millions of new textbooks have been printed and distributed, and teachers' salaries are far higher than under the former regime."[66]

Yet in October 2004, Mary Ann Zehr reported in *Education Week* a very different version of progress on CAII's rebuilding of Iraq's education system as schools reopened in Iraq since the U.S. invasion in March 2003. "Results of a ministry survey of schools released this fall show that more than 7,000 of Iraq's 11,000 primary schools either don't have a sewage system at all or don't have one that is operating properly, and that more than 4,000 primary schools have leaking roofs. The survey also estimates that 32,000 additional classrooms are needed."[67] Despite the Bush administration's No Child Left Behind emphasis on "accountability" of schools, teachers, and students, USAID was hardly forthcoming in response to requests for information on CAII's performance after the company's first year of operating in Iraq.

> Subcontractors to Creative Associates say they've been told by the USAID not to speak with the news media. In addition, the international-development agency won't release documents showing how either Creative Associates or Bechtel National Inc., a San Francisco–based company that was contracted to

repair schools, performed. In a March 25 letter, a USAID official justified the rejection of a Freedom of Information Act request for such documents filed by *Education Week* by writing, "Release of this deliberative-process information to the public could hamper the exchange of honest and open communications and thus adversely interfere with our agency's contract-monitoring activities.[68]

In fact, the secrecy of the performance on the first contract followed evasion of bidding protocol. Planning for CAII's involvement in rebuilding education in Iraq appears to have begun in November 2002 with a meeting between top executive Frank Dall and USAID.[69] On March 4, 2003, USAID invited five companies, including CAII, to bid on a project called Revitalization of Iraqi Schools and Stabilization of Education (RISE). "Of the five companies invited to bid on the multi-million dollar contract, only Creative had a representative at the November meeting, and it was the only company that submitted a proposal. In a subcontracting plan dated March 7, 2003, Creative listed three of the other five companies USAID invited to bid as possible subcontractors."[70] On March 26, CAII won the contract, and Frank Dall was named the project director. In June 2003, USAID conducted an internal investigation and concluded that only one of the five bidders (CAII) had been invited to the initial discussions with USAID and that procedures had not been followed in awarding the contract. Senator Joseph Lieberman of Connecticut reviewed the investigation and announced that there was "essentially no competitive bidding at all."[71] Congressional critics of the no-bid contracting say that it "allows the administration to reward friendly companies, prevents Congress from exercising its authority over spending, and may result in higher costs to taxpayers."[72]

In CAII's first year, the Research Triangle Institute formed educational policy.[73] CAII also did a survey to discover student–teacher ratios and then put together and distributed student kits with pens, pencils, erasers, and notebooks and the USAID logo on the kit. CAII's Web site features a photograph of these kits not being received by students in Iraq but rather being manufactured by a woman in a Chinese factory. CAII hired Iraqi companies to make furniture for the schools and gave out grant money to set up PTA-style organizations. While CAII arranged for the printing and delivery of textbooks, in the first year, USAID paid UNESCO $10 million to print 8.6 million math and science textbooks, and money from the United Nations "oil for food" program paid UNICEF to print 44.5 million textbooks for all other subjects. Andrew Natsios of USAID announced at a State Department briefing that a group including the Coalition Provisional Authority, the Ministry of Education, UNESCO, and UNICEF was "working on redoing the textbooks, which were full of vitriol and Baathist party propaganda."[74] "Redoing the textbooks" appears to have involved little more than selective censorship.

> Those textbooks are newly printed versions of the ones that Iraqi students used prior to the U.S.-led war in Iraq, minus references to ousted President Saddam Hussein or his Baath Party, which was edited out by Iraqi educators. Iraq's minister of education, Dr. Ala'din Alwan, said this month that Iraqi educators won't rewrite Iraq's textbooks until after the country's curriculum is revised, which he estimates will take two or three years.[75]

The delay in remaking the textbook content and curriculum belies the political nature of schooling. With the future of Iraq's government, ideology, and the duration of the occupation uncertain, the texts cannot render a verdict on even recent history let alone represent religion, politics, and cultural values. Nearly all of the popular press coverage of the remaking of Iraqi textbooks falsely suggested that the texts would be scrubbed of ideology and then be politically neutral. A *Washington Post* article went so far as to blame the insurgency on Saddam Hussein's textbooks. Such claims are important in the ways they deny the extensive political and historical education in the history of Western imperialism that, as Rashid Khalidi suggests, is a part of popular education in Iraq, which happens not just in the schools but also in the home, in the streets, and in the mosque.[76] The cleansing of such a history from the new texts and delinking the legacy of the earlier British imperialism from present-day occupation will certainly be a political agenda sponsored by USAID and the World Bank, which participate in the newest incarnation of American-led imperialism.

For the second year of the U.S. occupation, the World Bank joined educational rebuilding, offering $40 million for printing the same textbooks and $59 million for school rebuilding. Money originates with World Bank member countries, including the United States. The involvement of the World Bank in educational rebuilding is best understood in relation to its long-standing conditions on lending that aims at private-sector development through accelerated privatization and liberalization.[77]

For the second CAII contract, the role of the company shifted. In an article titled "Iraq Gets Approval to Control Destiny of School System" (imagine an article that said "Iraq Gets Approval to Control Energy Resources"), *Education Week* quoted the Iraqi minister of education, a former World Health Organization (WHO) official, saying that although USAID would continue to play a role in the education rebuilding, control was shifting from the Coalition Provisional Authority to the ministry.

Simply in terms of "effective delivery of educational services," the performance of CAII is questionable. Though by April 2004 USAID had refused to release information on CAII's performance in its first year in Iraq, Williamson M. Evers, a research fellow of the conservative Hoover Institution who worked with the company, gave CAII a poor evaluation. Though praising the company for effectively delivering school materials and furniture to schools and conducting a needs assessment, "All the other things in the contract that had to do with the longer-term development of the Education Ministry—and what is called capacity building—were not done well,' he contended. The work 'was poor, sloppy, had a lack of follow-though, and a lack of perseverance and persistence.'"[78] For the second contract, CAII dropped American University, American Islamic Congress, and RTI International while adding new subcontractors.

In April 2004, CAII withdrew most of its international staff from Iraq for security reasons. Nidhal Kadhim was an office manager for a CAII subcontractor, Iraq Foundation. One of six Iraqi professionals hired by CAII to advise the Ministry of Education, Kadhim criticized CAII for hiring too few Iraqis under the first contract. In fact, the USAID contract did not obligate CAII to hire any Iraqis. Referring to the company's teacher training project in the first year, Kadhim stated, "They took the whole project to themselves, and it was they who were doing all the materials and doing the training and preparing the materials. ... It would have been good to have local staff help with the preparation of the materials."[79]

The inefficient delivery of educational services appears inextricably linked to the use of private for-profit corporations. According to Farshad Rastegar, CEO of Los Angeles–based Relief International, which has built and repaired schools in Iraq, the failure to utilize nonprofits and instead to use private companies has wasted U.S. federal government money. While 27 cents of every dollar spent on the rebuilding generally has gone for intended projects, according to the Center for Strategic and International Studies, 30 percent is paying for security. Rastegar's group claims to spend only 1 percent on security: "We're not out there in big cars that say, 'I'm an expat, come and attack me.' We're not mixing with the military side of the operation. We're not identified with that."[80]

A Freedom of Information Act request found that CAII was getting $56.5 million for two years plus another $52 million possible during that period, plus potentially $82.6

million if the contract extends beyond two years. That means that if CAII makes the full $190 million, then the odds are that more than $60 million of it will not go for education at all but for security—most of which is being conducted for profit by private security corporations like Blackwater and Dyncorp. And based on the trend of reconstruction spending generally, less than what is spent on security will go to education. Is the expensive for-profit educational rebuilding worth the extra money? "The contract says the purpose of education reconstruction last school year was 'to normalize basic education in Iraq following a conflict,' but the new contract 'focuses on quality and access.' To provide that 'quality,' the contract says, schools will incorporate 'democratic practices in the classroom' and develop students' learning and critical-thinking skills."[81] Much popular press writing on educational rebuilding in Iraq suggests that the emphasis on "democratic education" comes as the basic needs of Iraq's children have yet to be met. As tens of millions of dollars are wasted on security to keep private U.S. companies controlling the rebuilding, the status of the youngest and most vulnerable Iraqis is perilous.

In the summer of 2004, with more than 40 percent of Iraqis below the age of fourteen, UNICEF found that infant mortality rates doubled since 1989 just before the first U.S. invasion and the decade of U.S.-led sanctions. "The mortality rate for children under age 5 is two and a half times its 1989 level. . . . Children suffer an average of nearly 15 episodes of diarrhea per year, up from 3.8 in 1990, and typhoid cases have spiked from 2240 to 27,000 in the same period."[82] At the beginning of the 2004–2005 school year, 5.7 million Iraqi children were expected to attend school, yet a national survey showed seven thousand of the eleven thousand primary schools did not have a functional sewage system, and four thousand primary schools have leaking roofs—conditions hardly conducive to children's health.

The point here is not that democratic educational ideals are at odds with these health conditions and that one must choose one or the other. Any democracy requires the health of citizens expected to govern themselves. Rather, the point is that proclamations about spreading democracy are hard to believe from the Iraqi perspective as the same people behind the alleged democracy promotion programs have been behind the two invasions, the aerial bombardment, and the devastating decade of sanctions that are estimated to have killed as many as one million Iraqi children directly or indirectly. What is more, the declared intent of democratic education can only make sense in relation to the conditions for democratic governance in Iraq more broadly. The Abu Ghraib prison situation, attempts to control the outcome of elections in ways favorable to U.S. interests, and the essential theft of Iraqi national wealth for the enrichment of multinational oil companies and for the strategic aims of the United States seem at odds with an honest effort at democracy promotion. Why the United States would opt for a private company under USAID such as CAII to execute education rebuilding despite the massive monetary waste of using a private contractor, despite the desperate dying children, and despite the massive oil wealth beneath the schools—this can only be understood as being about the retention of U.S. control over the outcome of the education system. Such an agenda is engineered for shifting power and profit to the private sector and retaining U.S. control over Iraqi civil society to implement such an agenda rather than about the will or welfare of the Iraqi people. What is more, if the aim of democratic education is the development of a more democratic society, then how should one understand democratic education projects as they are being enacted while democracy is being subverted in a number of other ways? That is, political, economic, and cultural control is being manipulated by the United States rather than being controlled by the Iraqi people.

Most pertinent here, the declaration of building "democratic education" can only be understood in relation to other declared aims of CAII's second contract. These other aims involve privatization. In April 2004, Zehr reported that CAII had been awarded a second contract from USAID with a different mission from that of the first contract. The first contract called for CAII to distribute furniture and materials to schools, train about thirty-three thousand teachers in "student-centered" educational methods, administer a survey to evaluate the needs of secondary schools, create accelerated learning programs for six hundred students, distribute grants for repairs to schools, and establish an information management system for the Ministry of Education.[83]

The second contract appears to set the stage for privatization of the Iraqi education system through "strengthening a decentralized education structure."[84] Such "decentralization" would foster a goal that USAID makes explicit on its Web site: "public-private partnerships."[85] The model for this appears to be the growing U.S. charter school movement that the federal government of the United States has supported with billions of dollars. Charters are the spearhead of public school privatization as more than three-quarters of new charters are opened by for-profits.[86] Domestically in the United States, one of the three major thrusts of No Child Left Behind is charter school promotion. The charter movement, following the ideals of neoliberal economic policy, emphasizes decentralization, deregulation, experimentation, involvement of the private for-profit sector, the undermining of teachers unions and local democratically elected school councils, and the handing of management over to business groups. Though the U.S. media has largely failed to pick up on the attempts to remake education on the current conservative educational reforms, the Assyrian International News Agency reports that a new crop of private for-profit schools are being opened in Iraq. Saddam Hussein had nationalized education in 1973, and Iraq was regarded as having one of the best education systems in the Middle East, with full gender inclusion, free to all, fostering 80 percent literacy, and a secular curriculum that did not require non-Muslims to partake in religious instruction. The wars with Iran that the

United States fueled from both sides, the Gulf War, and the decade of U.S.-led UN sanctions destroyed the educational system, with the 2003 U.S. invasion being the final straw. The USAID agenda for education in Iraq and around the world involves promoting "public-private partnerships."

> Certifying private schools is a way to add classrooms without tapping public coffers, [Interim Minister of Education] Allaq said. After years of surviving on subsidies, "The citizen is realizing that not everything can be provided by the government," he said. Private schools also received a boost because some of the American advisers sent to work with Iraq's transitional government had ties to the U.S. charter school movement and supported more local control of Iraqi schools.[87]

Allaq's parroting of the neoliberal U.S. justification for educational privatization is hard to fathom when one considers the amount of money being allocated for military, policing, and other repressive measures that are principally necessary because of the continuing U.S. military presence.

> For the new contract, the request for proposals focuses on the establishment of 162 model schools across Iraq that will exemplify good teaching methods and on the development of a television program for early childhood education. It also calls for the contractor to provide technical assistance to the staff of the Ministry of Education and direct a small-grants program for local communities. The new contract, expected to be signed by the end of May, will likely be worth $55 million, with another $95 million in funding possible, according to Dick L. McCall, the senior vice president for programs for Creative Associates.[88]

Though the noncompetitive bidding between the federal government and a for-profit corporation does raise important questions about corruption and how the public sector is being used to enrich a tiny elite in the private sector, this issue tends to eclipse a more fundamental one. Namely, the broader issue appears to be the role of military destruction and reconstruction as a form of neocolonialism—a way to justify the privatization agenda.

> "We used to have vulgar colonialism," says Shalmali Guttal, a Bangalore-based researcher with Focus on the Global South. "Now we have sophisticated colonialism, and they call it 're-construction.'" ... If anything, the stories of corruption and incompetence [in rebuilding] serve to mask this deeper scandal: the rise of a predatory form of disaster capitalism that uses the desperation and fear created by catastrophe to engage in radical social and economic engineering.[89]

It is just this radical social and economic engineering that appears to be the real story that educators committed to democratic ideals need to pay attention to, as media coverage of this issue appears nearly nonexistent. As in the domestic debates over corruption and efficient delivery of for-profit educational services (like The Edison Schools), the preponderance of press coverage focusing on fair business practices conceals the broader implications that privatization of public education has for a democratic society. Privatization of public education shifts control over public institutions to private hands, thereby undermining the role public education plays as a democratic public sphere, as a space for public deliberation over values, meanings, and matters of public import. Privatization of public education also redefines the very meaning of the public in private terms by treating a service that matters for the whole society as a consumable commodity that matters only for the individual consuming unit. Privatization also redefines public citizens as private consumers.

As in the case of election intervention and media reform initiatives, democratic education proposals appear to be principally about fostering state-backed ideological institutions conducive to the expansion of capitalist democracy or what Robinson calls polyarchy. Privatization and decentralization of public schooling in Iraq appear to follow the model of the United States under No Child Left Behind that expands federal control under the guise of local control while actually undermining local institutions such as teachers unions and democratically elected school councils that ensure local democratic control. In the United States, such projects have hardly promoted democracy as locales find themselves forced to follow federal guidelines for curriculum, remediation, and what constitutes legitimate knowledge and pedagogical practices, while extending punitive power of the state. The U.S. model merges neoliberal and neoconservative ideals: neoliberalism shifts educational values to market language and logic, conflating politics with economy and treating citizens as educational consumers. Charter schools fit the market logic, offering parents and students consumer choice while calling for schools to operate as entrepreneurial endeavors. The neoconservative recourse to the nation-state and the drive for total state control merges with neoliberalism's funding of the repressive functions of the state and undermining of the caregiving functions of the state. These funding trends are mutually enforcing; as the social safety net is destroyed, the state appears more justified in shifting capital into repressive measures. As long as the United States oversees and influences the new Iraqi Ministry of Education, and USAID and the World Bank continue to rebuild, U.S. models of control can be expected to be followed.

What cannot be forgotten is that the functions of public schools, public or private, in this context are (1) to teach skills and know-how that are economically useful for the particular kind of corporate capitalist economy Iraq will have, and (2) to teach skills and know-how in specific ways that are ideologically conducive to the reproduction of social relationships compatible with maintenance of capital accumulation by a transnational capitalist class. The latter includes forging dispositions, values, and identities conducive to capitalist democracy and a globalized consumer culture. Mechanisms of formal democracy promoted by democracy promotion projects are more conducive to corporate globalization than would be projects designed to foster democratic control over the means of production, democratic decision making over consumption, or democratic control over meaning-making technologies (schools, media, religion) that would shift power away from for-profit institutions and toward public control. Educators and cultural workers committed to such genuinely democratic shifts in control ought to not only oppose the U.S. occupation but also understand that the authoritarian privatization trends of the "new imperialism" and "disaster capitalism" can be identified operating not just in the "nonintegrating gap" but also in those power centers in the nations waging imperial war. The struggles for the fate of U.S. urban schools can no longer be seen apart from the motives for war on the Middle East and the rest of the world.

Notes

1. See Irvin Stelzer, "Introduction," in *The Neocon* Reader, ed. Irwin Stelzer (New York: Grove, 2004). The vision of remaking the world on the singular American model is clearly stated in the opening of the *National Security Strategy of the United States,* available at www.whitehouse.gov. The publication of *The Neocon Reader* was launched with an event covered by C-SPAN television and included lectures by William Kristol and Irvin Stelzer. The early plans for the reformulation of U.S. national security strategy can be found on the neoconservative Project for a New American Century Web site.
2. Despite repeated assertions by the Bush administration that the invasion of Iraq in March 2003 was part of the war on terrorism, no credible links have been found between the Islamist political movement Al Qaeda and the Iraq of Saddam Hussein. Osama bin Laden and Saddam Hussein were bitter enemies with incompatible ideological convictions. The admission by the Bush administration that no weapons of mass destruction could be

found in Iraq revealed as false the original justification for the war, which was the immediate security of the United States. This makes the war an illegal act within international law. In the buildup to war and since the invasion, the justifications for war by the administration and the news media have been interchangeably security, democratic nation building, moral imperative, and paternal revenge. In the context of education, these interchangeable justifications have been well documented on Megan Boler's Web site, Critical Media Literacy and War.

3. Jackie Spinner, "Questions Raised about Iraq Contract," *Washington Post,* June 13, 2003, E2; David Morris, "Criticism Grows of No-Bid Work for Iraq Reconstruction," *Congress Daily,* April, 16, 2003, 3.

4. This is detailed in Pratap Chatterjee, *Iraq, Inc.: A Profitable Occupation* (New York: Seven Stories Press, 2004). See also Christian Parenti, "Fables of the Reconstruction," *The Nation,* August 30–September 6, 2004, 16–19.

5. "War Profiteers" is how corporate watchdog group Corp Watch described the rebuilding contractors.

6. Christian Parenti describes the rebuilding generally this way.

7. "Windfalls of War" is the label provided by the Center for Public Integrity.

8. Stelzer, "Introduction."

9. Susanne Soederberg, "American Empire and Excluded States: The Millennium Challenge Account and the Shift to Pre-emptive Development," *Third World Quarterly* 25, no. 2: 281. Pentagon planner Thomas P. M. Barnett celebrates the "Pentagon's New Map," *Esquire,* March 2003, as a plan for global integration under the rules of corporate-dominated global trade agreements and organizations.

10. See David Harvey, *The New Imperialism* (Oxford: Oxford University Press, 2003), and Giovanni Arrighi, "Hegemony Unravelling," *New Left Review* 32 (March–April 2005).

11. William I. Robinson has written extensively and importantly on the U.S. foreign policy shift away from support for and promotion of authoritarian regimes and toward promotion of what he terms "polyarchy," forms of democracy that ratify elite rule through formal democratic processes while averting popular rule and control and ensuring market economies more effectively than authoritarianism. See, for example, William I. Robinson,

Promoting Polyarchy: Globalization, U.S. Intervention, and Hegemony (Cambridge: Cambridge University Press, 1995), and William I. Robinson, "Globalization, the World System, and 'Democracy Promotion' in U.S. Foreign Policy," *Theory and Society* 25 (1996): 615–65.

12. See, for example, Chatterjee, *Iraq, Inc.*

13. I have taken up the relationships between recent educational reform and privatization in *The Edison Schools: Corporate Schooling and the Assault on Public Education* (New York: Routledge, 2005).

14. As David Harvey and Giovanni Arrighi note, if the prominent figures in the Clinton administration were the finance people such as Rubin and Summers, then they are the military people in the Bush White House, such as Rumsfeld, Cheney, and the neoconservative staff of hawks like Wolfowitz, Perle, and others. See Harvey, *The New Imperialism,* and Giovanni Arrighi, "Hegemony Unravelling."

15. Robinson, "Globalization," 619.

16. Leslie Sklair, "The Culture-Ideology of Consumerism in the Third World," in *Sociology of the Global System* (Baltimore: Johns Hopkins University Press, 1991).

17. Henry Giroux has importantly and correctly criticized the theoretical shortcomings of Althusser's project in the context of education. See especially Henry A. Giroux, *Theory and Resistance in Education: A Pedagogy for the Opposition* (South Hadley, Mass.: Bergin & Garvey, 1983), and Stanley Aronowitz and Henry A. Giroux, *Education Still under Siege* (Westport, Conn.: Bergin & Garvey, 1994), for these crucial criticisms. Despite Althusser's limitations, his insights about state power offer distinct tools for the present historical juncture.

18. This is not to discount the systematic ways the United States waged war on the third world from the end of World War II to the present, particularly in Central America, but from the end of the Vietnam War and the coinciding rise of neoliberalism.

19. See Kenneth J. Saltman and David Gabbard, *Education as Enforcement: The Militarization and Corporatization of Schools* (New York: Routledge, 2003). From public schools made into military academies, to JROTC, to a rising punitive culture of discipline, this phenomenon is only increasing, particularly as the U.S. military becomes desperate to fill its ranks.

20. Harvey, *The New Imperialism,* 141–42.

21. See Carl Boggs, *Imperial Delusions* (Lanham, Md.: Rowman & Littlefield, 2005); Henry Giroux, *Proto-Fascism in America: Neoliberalism and the Demise of Democracy* (Bloomington, Ind.: Phi Delta Kappa Educational Foundation, 2004); Henry Giroux, *Abandoned Generation: Democracy beyond the Culture of Fear* (New York: Palgrave Macmillan, 2004); Kenneth Saltman and David Gabbard, eds., *Education as Enforcement: The Militarization and Corporatization of Schools* (New York: Routledge Falmer, 2003). The overthrow of Saddam Hussein's authoritarian Iraq is in part about its replacement by a system of mechanisms designed for authoritarian corporate control, not its replacement by a participatory democratic system. This is confirmed across the political spectrum as Pentagon planner Thomas P. M. Barnett celebrates the "Pentagon's New Map" as a plan for global integration under the rules of corporate-dominated global trade agreements and organizations, an understanding shared by the *New York Times'* Thomas Friedman in his "Flat Earth" thesis (*The World Is Flat: A Brief History of the Twenty-first Century* [New York: Farrar, Straus & Giroux, 2005]), or assailed on the left by Vandana Shiva, "The Polarised World of Globalization," *ZNet,* May 28, 2005, among others.

22. The surging culture of religious right-wing populism, irrational New Age mysticism, and endless conspiracy theorizing appear to be symptoms of a cultural climate in which neoliberal market fundamentalism has come into crisis as both economic doctrine and ideology. Within this climate, private for-profit knowledge-making institutions, including schools and media, are institutionally incapable of providing a language and criticism that would enable rational interpretation necessary for political intervention. Irrationalism is the consequence. Not-too-distant history suggests that this can lead in systematically deadly directions.

23. The Center for Public Integrity, "Windfalls of War: Creative Associates International Inc.," http://www.publicintegrity.org/wow/bio.aspx?act=pro&ddlC=11.

24. The Center for Public Integrity, "Windfalls of War"; Jackie Spinner, "Iraq: Operation Iraqi Education," *Washington Post,* April 21, 2003.

25. The Center for Public Integrity, "Windfalls of War."

26. Mary Ann Zehr, "Schools Open in Iraq, after Two-Week Delay," *Education Week,* October 13, 2004, 6–7.

27. This is how the Center for Public Integrity describes her teaching past.
28. The Center for Public Integrity, "Windfalls of War."
29. Spinner, "Iraq."
30. Vice President Cheney headed Halliburton and continued to benefit economically from the company. Halliburton's subsidiaries include Bechtel. Condoleezza Rice worked for Chevron, which named an oil tanker after her. Iraq rebuilding administration shifted to the National Security Agency under Rice, and Chevron received early large oil contracts following the invasion.
31. Staff, "The Spoils of War: Cleaning Up," *The Economist,* April 3, 2003.
32. Joel Russell, "Public Policy Benefits Providers," *Hispanic Business* 25, no. 6 (June 2003).
33. For my use of the term *imperialism,* I draw on the work of Harvey, *The New Imperialism*; Douglas Stokes's essays; Ellen Meiskins Wood, *Empire of Capital* (New York: Verso, 2005); Michael Parenti's *Against Empire* (San Francisco: City Lights Books, 1995); as well as Hannah Arendt's *The Origins of Totalitarianism* (New York: Harcourt, Brace & World, 1966). These more and less nuanced versions of empire emphasize that while the nation-state may be weakened by the deregulatory rules of the post-Fordist economy, they emphasize the tensions between the extranational interests of a transnational capitalist class and the wielding of national power for economic advantage by military action against other nations. Parenti writes, "By 'imperialism' I mean the process whereby the dominant politico-economic interests of one nation expropriate for their own enrichment the land, labor, raw materials, and markets of another people." The term *imperialism,* long derided in mass media as little more than a loony left marker of conspiracy theory and rejected as illegitimate scholarship in academia, has only recently again begun to be taken seriously across the political spectrum as a traditional conservative isolationism joins progressive and radical left criticism of the neoconservative plans for U.S. global military control.
34. The Center for Public Integrity, "Windfalls of War," 5.
35. Spinner, "Iraq."
36. Spinner, "Iraq."
37. William Blum, *Killing Hope* (Monroe, Maine: Common Courage, 2004), 290.

Chapter 2

Chapter 2

38. Blum, *Killing Hope*, 293.

caii.com/CAIIStaff/Dashboard_GIROAdminCAIIStaff/Dashboard_
CAIIAdminDatabase/highlights1.htm.

56. USAID Haiti/Creative Associates International, "Haiti Media Assistance," appendix.

57. "Who's Who among Haiti's New Rulers?" *OneWorld.net.*

58. Paul Farmer, "The Flooding and the Coup: An Interview with Paul Farmer," *St. Petersburg Times,* June 14, 2004.

59. Alice Blanchet, "Opening of the Haiti Democracy Project," November 20, 2002, Haiti Democracy Project, Web page item #359, http://www.haitipolicy.org.

60. Nancy San Martin, "Haitians' Growing Discontent with Aristide May Force U.S. to Act," *Miami Herald,* August 19, 2002.

61. San Martin, "Haitians' Growing Discontent."

62. Farmer, "The Flooding and the Coup."

63. Naomi Klein, "The Rise of Disaster Capitalism," *The Nation,* May 2, 2005, 10.

64. Though the Brookings Institution is regarded as a politically "centrist" think tank, it is clearly in favor of conservative educational privatization plans and counts as fellows a number of outspoken advocates of for-profit public schooling, such as John Chubb, the chief education officer of The Edison Schools. This is discussed in Kenneth J. Saltman, *The Edison Schools: Corporate Schooling and the Assault on Public Education* (New York: Routledge, 2005).

65. "Foreign Affairs: Iraq by the Numbers," *Atlantic Monthly,* July/August 2004, 60.

66. "Foreign Affairs."

67. Zehr, "Schools Open in Iraq.

68. Zehr, "Iraq Gets Approval to Control Destiny of School System," *Education Week,* April 14, 2004, 1.

69. Center for Public Integrity, "Windfalls of War," 2.

70. Center for Public Integrity, "Windfalls of War," 2.

71. Center for Public Integrity, "Windfalls of War," 2.

72. David Morris, "Criticism Grows of No-Bid Work for Iraq Reconstruction," *CongressDaily,* April 16, 2003, 3.

73. CAII subcontracted Iraq rebuilding work with three of the four companies that were invited to bid but did not. These included Research Triangle Institute and DevTech Systems Inc. Research Triangle in turn subcontracts to CAII. CAII also subcontracts to American University, American Manufacturers Export

Group, Booz Allen Hamilton, and Camp Dresser & McKee International and two nonprofits led by Iraqi expatriates, American Islamic Congress and the Iraqi Foundation.

74. Center for Public Integrity, "Windfalls of War," 4.

75. Mary Ann Zehr, "World Bank Joins School Rebuilding Campaign," *Education Week,* April 14, 2004, 27.

76. See Rashid Khalidi, *Footprints of Empire* (New York: New Press, 2004).

77. See Steven J. Klees, "The Implications of the World Bank's Private Sector (PSD) Strategy for Education: Increasing Inequality and Inefficiency," January 15, 2002, available at Citizens Network on Essential Services (www.servicesforall.org).

78. Zehr, "Iraq Gets Approval," 3.

79. Mary Ann Zehr, "Creative Associates Gets New Iraq Contract," *Education Week,* July14, 2004, 17.

80. Zehr, "Schools Open in Iraq," 2.

81. Zehr, "Schools Open in Iraq," 2.

82. Valerie J. Brown, " Reconstructing the Environment in Iraq," *Environmental Health Perspectives* 112, no. 8 (June 2004): A464.

83. Zehr, "Iraq Gets Approval," 1.

84. Zehr, "Creative Associates," 17.

85. USAID's Web site has several links to a number of programs highlighting its emphasis on privatizing public-sector provision. There are explicit programs for development of private-sector involvement in education, while the neoliberal ideology informing the perspective of USAID celebrates liberalization and privatization of the service sector.

86. Alex Molnar, Glen Wilson, and Daniel Allen, "Profiles of For-Profit Educational Management Companies: Fifth Annual Report" (Tempe, Ariz.: Commercialism in Education Research Unit at Arizona State University, January 2003), available at www.schoolcommercialism.org.

87. Robin Fields, "Iraq Ministry of Education Withholds Approval for Private Assyrian School," *Los Angeles Times,* February 9, 2005, http://www.aina.org/news/2005029101342.htm.

88. Zehr, "Iraq Gets Approval," 1.

89. Klein, "The Rise of Disaster Capitalism," 9.

3
Renaissance 2010 and No Child
Left Behind

Breaking and Taking Schools and Communities

ᐧᢀ

The prior chapters illustrate how natural and unnatural disasters have been used for the radical social and economic engineering of schooling by the political Right. Long-desired reforms that the Right has failed to achieve through properly political means, it has achieved by seizing on emergency conditions. In the U.S. Gulf Coast and in Iraq, the Right is achieving multiple forms of privatization by taking advantage of exceptional circumstances. Business elites are being enriched at the expense of the public sector through for-profit no-bid contracting, antiunionism, decentralization, authoritarian governance, vouchers, charter schools, and the support of EMOs. Privatizing schooling through the war in Iraq may seem like an exceptional circumstance, but it follows from the tendency of neoliberalism toward the use of force to open markets globally and to annihilate public institutions. Hurricane Katrina may as well seem like an exceptional circumstance, but it allowed for a wide-scale privatization scheme that was already under way. Considering the imperial foreign policy now dominating Washington and the ravages of global warming, time will tell just how exceptional these circumstances are. This chapter illustrates how this mode of achieving privatization by taking advantage of disaster is not an exception limited to unique situations.

This chapter focuses on Chicago's nationally leading reform model Renaissance 2010 and its relationship to the most significant and powerful school reform legislation, the federal No Child Left Behind act (NCLB). I show that capitalizing on disaster is at the very center of educational reform in the United States. In this sense, what appears as unique in Iraq and the U.S. Gulf must be understood as part of a broader and dominant contemporary pattern of making disastrous schooling conditions and then declaring public schools as "failed" and ripe for privatization. What is central to dominant and leading school reform is how business and the political Right are capitalizing on disaster. That is, they are capitalizing on the long-standing failure to publicly invest in public schools and public housing, and they are making investment opportunities from the disastrous conditions they have participated in producing.

In what follows here, I (1) discuss the relationships between Renaissance 2010 and NCLB; (2) elaborate on the privatization agenda of Renaissance 2010 by showing how it is being pushed by the long-standing and concerted efforts of business groups as well as the neoliberal ideology they embrace; (3) show how Renaissance 2010 belies a racialized economic grab to profit from public housing and public schooling and to seize desirable real estate—public school closings and reopenings are a tool in displacing the poor and taking land; and (4) illustrate how Renaissance 2010 also exemplifies a shift in educational and political governance in a highly undemocratic direction.

Renaissance 2010 participates in producing new disasters: (1) far fewer schools for the displaced as they are shuffled from one closing school to the next; (2) far less public housing available for residents as they are displaced, moved off public housing rolls, and subjected to the whims of the market; (3) far less democratic governance over public schools and public housing as democratic governance shifts away from the public and toward business; and (4) the redirection of public resources to the rich in both schooling and housing.

The first and second chapters illustrated how disaster is being taken advantage of to force through the privatization agenda. This chapter shows how the long-standing production of disastrous public housing and public schooling in Chicago and nationally is being used to justify privatization. In addition, this chapter shows that the new privatization in turn produces new disasters for the residents being displaced from their schools and homes. To begin, I illustrate this trend by focusing on one transformation in Chicago: Oakwood Shores.

From Madden Wells to Oakwood Shores

On the South Side of Chicago, three joined public housing developments have been almost completely torn down following the Chicago Housing Authority's (CHA) reinvention at the turn of the millennium. The developments, created under President Franklin Roosevelt to be high-quality public housing exclusively for African Americans in an era of explicit segregation, were Madden Park, the Ida B. Wells development, and the Clarence Darrow Homes, two of which were named for great Chicago civil rights activists. In 2003, they together provided housing for 2,200 public housing residents, not including the 479 units of the Darrow Homes that had previously been razed in 2000.[1] The complex sits on desirable lakefront land. In its place the city, CHA, and HUD provided millions of dollars to private investors to develop a mixed-income community called Oakwood Shores. Oakwood Shores is an ambitious project that aims to develop over ninety-four acres of land by 2009.[2] Under the plan, the final housing complex will combine market-rate sales of condos, townhomes, and single-family homes and include rentals of 1,000 public housing units, 680 "affordable" units, and 1,320 market rate units. The market-rate properties are selling at as much as $535,000.[3] The new mixed-income development has a fraction of the public housing formerly available, and the new public housing is highly exclusive, requiring extensive background checks for work history, credit checks, drug tests, and other impossible hurdles for those with the direst housing needs.[4] Under "tough screening rules for public housing tenants including a work requirement ... just 38 percent of the 400 families screened so far are eligible for Oakwood."[5] CHA reports about 150,000 people waiting for public housing in 2005, with a third of those earning less than 30 percent of area median income.[6]

The new development comes at a tremendous cost to the public by reducing public housing and providing massive public subsidies to investors: Phase I of this development resulted in 163 total units, of which only 63 must be maintained as public housing and only for 40 years; public financing for Phase I surpassed $20 million. The "master plan" slated for 2009 calls for 1,320, or nearly half, market-rate residences from a total of 3,000 units, 1,000 public housing, and 680 affordable.[7] The estimated and projected costs differ grossly from the actual costs. For Oakwood Shores, a $35 million grant was awarded by the federal Hope VI project alone, but actual development costs could exceed $100 million for the new community. Moreover, millions more dollars of equity were created for private investors by the sale of low-income housing tax credits that benefit large corporations. Corporations benefit by receiving a dollar-for-dollar credit on their federal income taxes for the millions they invest in the project. With the fees, administrative costs, and multilayered financing, the cost of the 163 units, only 63 of which are public housing, easily surpasses about $300,000 per unit, about a couple of hundred thousand dollars per unit more than the cost to the public had the CHA directly contracted to construct the units.

The public housing residents from Madden/Wells/Darrow were displaced from their homes and communities. Their elementary school, the George Donohue Elementary School, was closed. Under Renaissance 2010, its building was taken and given to the University of Chicago Charter School. The new school is being used as a selling point for prospective buyers of the half-million-dollar market-rate homes in the new community. It is also being used as a lure for the exclusive applications to the restricted public housing. The new school was given an exemption from the state to restrict its boundaries to the new community and not be open lottery, as charter schools are technically required to be. Consequently, the new school has a handpicked student body more representative of the privileged residents of the new developments. The children of those displaced from the destroyed public housing end up in overcrowded public schools with paltry resources, subject to the prospect of future high-stakes-testing-based closures and in the immediacy subject to high racial and class segregation.[8]

On May 23, 2006, the CEO of the lead developer of Oakwood Shores, Patrick Clancy, spoke before the House Government Reform Subcommittee on Federalism and the Census. In his talk, "Public Housing in the Competitive Market Place: Do Affordable and Public Housing Developments Benefit from Private Market and Other Financing Tools?" the first element of the project's vision was as follows:

> Charter Schools. Under the Mayor's plan for change in public education [Renaissance 2010], the University of Chicago has opened a pre-K to 8 charter school this past fall immediately adjacent to the new mixed-income housing we are creating. Attached to this Appendix is a table showing the dramatic progress in test results over the first months of operation of this school. New high quality public education for this mixed-income community is a central component of its long term strength. Our belief in its importance has us designing a complex financial plan that we hope will enable an additional charter high school to be created in the new community.

The Oakwood Shores example vividly illustrates a much broader coordinated assault on public schooling and public housing that undermines public goods and services while representing the private forces behind the destruction as saviors.

Renaissance 2010 illustrates a number of neoliberal reforms that seek to undermine welfare state provisions and replace them with market-based policies. Such neoliberal ideology includes a constant touting of the benefits of privatization and deregulation, a constant demonizing of public interventions and public protections in economic management, and a triumphalism that celebrates the unquestioned victory of the "free market" over all other forms of governance. Despite the antigovernment rhetoric, as this chapter shows, often such ideology is used to capture government power to redistribute public wealth to investors. The privatization of the public sector is evident in nearly every social domain: dismantling of Aid to Families with Dependent Children (AFDC) and the creation of "workfare"; the dismantling of public housing and its replacement with public-private-partnership, mixed-income housing; the erosion of universal public schooling and the ongoing push for privatization, vouchers, and charter schools; the assault on public parks that are being handed over to industry for exploitation; attempts to privatize Social Security; the corporatization of Medicare; vast outsourcing of the military as typified by Halliburton and Bechtel; and the privatization of eminent domain that redefines the public good through business development. These policy transformations are bolstered not merely by attempts of conservatives and neoliberals to slash social spending or, rather, to radically militarize social spending by shifting it into military and security pork-barrel spending. Privatization of public goods and services is also largely pushed forward by an onslaught of market-based public pedagogy, from reality television that imagines community through social Darwinian business competition to political discourse that describes political issues through the health of the stock market, to the overtaking of school policy discourse by the business language of efficiency, competition, achievement, and choice that naturalizes the business uses of schooling rather than through public language. Market-based pedagogy produces common sense about the best course of public action. Unfortunately this is a common sense that frequently fails to cohere with reality or with the public interest. This is all too apparent when it comes to both public housing and public schooling.

Renaissance 2010 and NCLB

In the summer of 2004, Mayor Richard Daley announced before the Commercial Club of Chicago a dramatic plan for the nation's third-largest public school system. Chicago's Renaissance 2010 plan targets at least 10 percent of the city system to dismantle a number of Chicago Public Schools and opens one hundred new experimental schools in areas slated for gentrification by the city and business groups. Renaissance 2010 was announced as a bold reform to improve "achievement" by the replacement of "failed" big schools with deregulated smaller schools. The new schools would be a mix of charter schools, "contract schools" (essentially more charter schools that get a new name to circumvent state limits on charters), and "performance schools." The plan was met with outrage by teachers, teachers unions, activists, scholars, and students as a grand privatization scheme that dismantles public schooling, fosters gentrification, undermines democratically elected local school councils, undermines teachers unions, and shifts school governance away from communities and toward business elites. News coverage of the announcement showed Daley receiving a standing ovation from the Civic Committee of the Commercial Club following the speech. Daley had not devised the plan. Rather his audience, the Commercial Club, a century-old group composed of the largest and most powerful corporations in the city, had provided the mayor with it. He repeated it back to them to thunderous applause. Business power in the city spoke through the mayor. And if anyone was unclear as to the agenda, they could listen to Andrew

J. McKenna, Civic Committee chairman of the Commercial Club, who gushed about Renaissance 2010, "Chicago is taking the lead across the nation in remaking urban education. No other major city has launched such an ambitious public school choice agenda."[9]

In addition to the Commercial Club, the Chicago Public Schools hired a corporate consulting firm, A. T. Kearney, to oversee the planning and development of Renaissance 2010. Its Web site reads,

> The planning committee brought together an array of stake-holders and outside experts to devise a new educational model. In the initial phase, a coalition of education experts and community leaders created a broad-stroke plan. With this big picture set, A. T. Kearney enlisted a pro-bono team to help CPS develop a transformation plan that would turn this vision into reality. Drawing on our program-management skills and our knowledge of best practices used across industries, we provided a private-sector perspective on how to address many of the complex issues that challenge other large urban education transformations.[10]

This private-sector perspective was bolstered by the appointment of former vice president of Bank One and CEO of the Chicago Board of Trade David Vitale to chief administrative officer of the Chicago Public Schools.

Through high-stakes accountability regimes, both Renaissance 2010 and NCLB set schools up to be declared "failed." No Child Left Behind makes impossible demands requiring public schools continually to make higher Adequate Yearly Progress (AYP) on test scores. A study of the Great Lakes region of the United States by educational policy researchers found that 85 to 95 percent of schools in that region would be declared "failed" by NCLB AYP measures by 2014.[11] These implications are national. Under NCLB, "The entire country faces tremendous failure rates, even under a conservative estimate with several forgiving assumptions."[12] Under NCLB, in order for Illinois, for example, to get much-needed federal

Title I funds, the school must demonstrate AYP. Each year Illinois has to get higher and higher standardized test scores in reading and math to make AYP. Illinois schools, and specifically Illinois schools already receiving the least funding and already serving the poorest students, are being threatened with (1) losing federal funds; (2) having to use scarce resources for underregulated and often unproven supplemental educational services (SESes; e.g., private tutoring), such as Newton, a spin-off company of the much-criticized for-profit Edison Schools; or (3) being punished, reorganized, or closed and reopened as a "choice" school (these include for-profit or nonprofit charter schools that do not have the same level of public oversight and accountability, that often do not have teachers unions, and that often have to struggle for philanthropic grants to operate). Many defenders of public education view remediation options 2 and 3 under NCLB as having been designed to undermine those public schools that have been underserved in the first place in order to justify privatization schemes.[13]

Public schools need help, investment, and public commitment. As Jonathan Kozol suggests in *The Shame of the Nation*,[14] those schools in communities facing the greatest adversity need the most investment. NCLB does just the opposite by punishing these schools and demanding that they have what it does not give. NCLB is setting up for failure not just Illinois public schools but public schools nationally by raising test-oriented thresholds without raising investment and commitment. NCLB itself appears to be a system designed to result in the declaration of wide-scale failure of public schooling to justify privatization.[15] Dedicated administrators, teachers, students, and schools are not receiving much-needed resources along with public investment in public services and employment in the communities where those schools are situated. What they are getting instead is threats.

The theoretically and empirically dubious underlying assumption of NCLB is that threats and pressure force teachers to teach what they ought to teach, force students to learn what they ought to learn. In terms of conventional measures of student achievement, Sharon Nichols, Gene Glass, and David Berliner found in their empirical study, *High-Stakes Testing and Student Achievement: Problems for the No Child Left Behind Act,* that "there is no convincing evidence that the pressure associated with high-stakes testing leads to any important benefits for students' achievement.... [The authors] call for a moratorium on policies that force the public education system to rely on high-stakes testing."[16] These authors find that high-stakes testing regimes do not achieve what they are designed to achieve. However, to think beyond efficacy to the underlying assumptions about "achievement," it is necessary to raise theoretical concerns. Theoretically, at the very least, the enforcement-oriented assumptions of NCLB fail to consider the limitations of defining "achievement" through high-stakes tests, fail to question what knowledge and whose knowledge constitute legitimate or official curricula that students are expected to master, and fail to interrogate the problematic assumptions of learning modeled on digestion or commodity acquisition (as opposed to dialogic, constructivist, or other approaches to learning). Moreover, such compartmentalized versions of knowledge and learning fail to comprehend how they relate to the broader social and political realities informing knowledge-making both in schools and in society generally. Like NCLB, Renaissance 2010 targets schools that have "failed" to meet Chicago accountability standards defined through high-stakes tests. Renaissance 2010, by closing and reopening schools, allows the newly privatized schools to circumvent NCLB AYP progress requirements, which makes the list of Chicago's "need improvement" schools shorter. This allows the city to claim improvement by simply redefining terms.

NCLB and Renaissance 2010 share a number of features, including not only a high-pressure model but also reliance on standardized testing as the ultimate measure of learning, threats to teacher job security and teachers unions, and a push for experimentation with unproven models, including privatization and charter schools, as well as a series of neoliberal assumptions and guiding language. For example, speaking of Renaissance 2010, Mayor Daley stated, "This model will generate competition and allow for innovation. It will bring in outside partners who want to get into the business of education."[17]

Beyond its similarities to NCLB, Renaissance 2010 is being hailed as a national model in its own right across the political spectrum. The Bill and Melinda Gates Foundation is the most heavily endowed philanthropy in history, worth about $80 billion, with projects in health and education. Its focus on school reform is guided by the neoliberal Democratic Leadership Council's Progressive Policy Institute. Though it offers no substance, argument, or evidence for why Renaissance 2010 should be replicated, the economically unmatched Gates Foundation praises Renaissance 2010 as a "roadmap" for other cities to follow.[18] As Pauline Lipman, a progressive urban education scholar at the University of Illinois of Chicago writes, Chicago's accountability scheme prior to NCLB and Renaissance 2010 has been a national model, while Renaissance 2010 itself stands as a national model of remediation in the form of privatization.

> If Chicago's accountability has laid the groundwork for privatization, Renaissance 2010 may signal what we can expect nationally as school districts fail to meet NCLB benchmarks. In fact, failure to make "adequate yearly progress" on these benchmarks, and the threat of a state takeover, is a major theme running through the Commercial Club's argument for school choice and charter schools. Business and political leaders seem to believe turning schools over to the market is a common sense solution to the problems in the schools.[19]

Both NCLB and Renaissance 2010 involve two stages of capitalizing on disaster. The first stage involves the historical underfunding and disinvestment in public schooling that have resulted in disastrous public school conditions. For those communities where these schools are located, it is the public and private sectors that have failed them. Although the corporate sector is usually represented not only in mass media but also in much conservative and liberal educational policy literature as coming to rescue the incompetent public sector from itself, as Dorothy Shipps points out in her book *School Reform, Corporate Style: Chicago 1880–2000,* the corporate sector in Chicago and around the nation has long been deeply involved in school reform, agenda setting, and planning in conjunction with other civic planning. As she asks, "if corporate power was instrumental in creating the urban public schools and has had a strong hand in their reform for more than a century, then why have those schools failed urban children so badly?"[20] Rather than engaging Shipps's historical question, my concern here is with the second stage of disaster—the new ways that this historical production of disastrous schooling is being capitalized on now through Renaissance 2010.[21] According to its proponents, Renaissance 2010 is a plan for renewal, excellence, and achievement. To its critics, it is a plan for displacement, insecurity, and the theft of public resources from the poor by the rich—it is insult and injury added to historical injury.

The Privatization of Public Housing in Chicago

Renaissance 2010 is NOT just a school plan. It is part of a much larger plan for gentrification and for moving out low-income African Americans and some Latinos from prime real estate areas. In fact from the city altogether. These are the areas where the proposed school closings are concentrated. Gentrification is a key element of making Chicago a global city of increasing inequality in housing, income, quality of life, and use of urban space. To put it simply, the land is valuable, the people are not.[22]

Chicago's high-rise public housing and the public schools serving them have suffered some of the worst neglect imaginable. Such housing projects as Cabrini-Green and the Robert Taylor Homes have a national reputation for squalid and violent living conditions. These housing projects, which are symptoms of the legacy of racialized class oppression in the United States, originate with white violence and reaction to historical attempts at racial integration. By the mid-twentieth century,

> Blacks still faced widespread employment discrimination. Stores in the Loop refused to hire African Americans as clerks. Black bus drivers, police officers, and firefighters were limited to positions serving their own community. Construction trades remained closed. Moreover, the second Great Migration made Chicago's already overcrowded slums even more dilapidated, as more and more people tried to fit into converted "kitchenette" and basement apartments in which heating and plumbing were poor, if functioning at all. Street crime in African American communities remained a low priority for Chicago's police, and violence, prostitution, and various other vices soared in black neighborhoods. When Elizabeth Wood, executive director of the Chicago Housing Authority (CHA), tried to ease the pressure in the overcrowded ghetto by proposing public housing sites in less congested areas elsewhere in the city in 1946, white residents reacted with intense and sustained violence. City politicians forced the CHA to keep the status quo, setting the stage for the development of Chicago's infamous high-rise projects, such as Cabrini-Green and the Robert Taylor Homes.[23]

Sustained and systematic neglect of high-rise public housing in Chicago and nationally resulted in crumbling infrastructures and chronic infestation by rodents and insects. Refusal to publicly invest in maintenance resulted in the city paving over the green space of Cabrini-Green with asphalt and wrapping the building with wire mesh. Transforming such facilities on the models of the prison, high-rise public housing symbolically functioned to let residents know their value in the eyes of those with power. As the city neglected to maintain housing, anyone who could moved out. Thus, public housing was made into a home of last resort for those with the least resources and options. Racial segregation, class oppression, and economic exclusion merged with public disinvestment, producing buildings with all of the most egregious effects of dire poverty, including epidemic levels of crime, gangs, police surveillance, ill health, hopelessness, despair, and depression. The historical disinvestment in public housing made it into a disaster akin to a war zone or a natural disaster. Despite and even because of these conditions, there is a strong sense of community on the part of residents. Yet the remedy dismembers community rather than investing in it. As Kozol recounts in his book *Savage Inequalities,*[24] such disastrous housing conditions are matched by a monumental failure to invest in public schooling.

Driving to Chicago's Cabrini-Green today, one finds the vestiges of the public housing complex that once housed twenty-five thousand units but has been gradually demolished building by building since the mid-1990s. Located between the city's Near North aptly named Gold Coast, the exclusive Old Town, and posh Lincoln Park neighborhoods, the remaining buildings sit on coveted land and are surrounded by encroaching new luxury condominium and townhome complexes (North Town Village, Renaissance North, Orchard Park, Old Town Square, etc.) that include shopping plazas catering to high-spending residents. Starbucks, dry cleaners, Blockbuster video stores, and banks inaccessible to most public housing residents sprout up around the new developments. Such private investment in well-equipped supermarkets and other retail was absent before. Instead, retail around the projects long preyed on the poor, charging more for groceries. Bad supermarkets charged a "poverty tax" of a 20 percent markup for most goods.

The high-end retail is not likely to be found where former residents of Cabrini will be forced to move. Although CHA claims that former residents are entitled to return to a redeveloped or rehabilitated unit, the reality is that very few return. This is because they are forced into the market with a housing voucher that depends on an accepting landlord, and when one is not found, tenants lose housing subsidy altogether, risking homelessness. Moreover, private managers impose stringent occupation restrictions, including credit checks, drug tests, and proof of full-time employment. Thus, the plan assaults those most in need of public housing, including the disabled, the elderly, and others unable to sustain full-time employment. Residents displaced by the CHA's "Plan for Transformation" are forced to other temporary neighborhoods and then must apply to get back home to the fraction of affordable public units in the new mixed-income developments, which are tightly restricted by the covenants dictated by real estate development companies. The public schools that served the residents of public housing are being closed in the new gilded communities and reopened mostly as charter schools meant to serve the new population and under control by the same business forces that have planned the urban transformations, not under control of the public housing residents who have resisted the plans as a scheme designed fundamentally to displace them from coveted real estate.

An early aspect of Renaissance 2010 was called "Mid-South," referring to a section of Chicago's South Side. A "tool for gentrifying certain Chicago neighborhoods,"[25] Mid-South called for closing twenty of twenty-two schools in that section of the city. Lipman elucidates the links between gentrification and the school closing plan of Renaissance 2010:

> As public housing is torn down and new condos and luxury town houses rise up, the city and the real estate developers are removing any traces of the people who once lived there. Closing the schools and then reopening them as new schools is a signal to future middle-class residents that the area is being "reborn." This has been a frequent theme in business and school leaders' statements in the press. When the agenda to "reinvent" Midsouth schools was first made public in the *Chicago Tribune,* on December 19, 2003, Terry Mazany, CEO of Chicago Community Trust and member of the planning team, described the connection between schools and development of the area this way: "[Bronzeville's] a great physical location,

so close to the lake and downtown," he said. "It's a delicate balance to pull something like this off. You can't do it just with the housing and retail development. You have to get the third leg and that's the schools."[26]

Although the city has backed off the Mid-South plan (for schools), Renaissance 2010 continues alongside citywide gentrification plans. The Metropolitan Planning Council Web site contains explicit charts that detail plans to close and reopen city schools in neighborhoods with current or planned mixed-income communities. The accompanying chart details the retail potential and unemployment in communities surrounding new mixed-income developments.[27]

Renaissance 2010 must be understood in relation to the long-standing decimation of public housing in Chicago. In the case of Chicago's public housing, the market logic produced a common sense that advocated the dismantling of public housing and the turning over of public housing development to the cooperation of real estate development companies and federal and local housing authorities. In 1999, the CHA fundamentally shifted its role in providing public housing. The stated goal of the Plan for Transformation was to reinvent public housing in Chicago by improving its appearance, quality, and culture. Under this plan, CHA drastically reduced its role in owning and directly providing housing for poor Chicagoans. Its new role largely involved facilitating public-private partnership projects by giving money and control to for-profit investors and developers. The new role hands public resources and property and governance to business under the guise of urban renewal. CHA is doing this with the explicit approval, encouragement, and financing of the Department of Housing and Urban Development. As public housing projects like the Robert Taylor Homes and Cabrini-Green are razed to the ground, far fewer public housing units are created in those communities in the new mixed-income developments.

Shortly after the Republican takeover of the House of Representatives, in 1995, Congress ended the "one-for-one replacement housing requirement" law requiring replacement of public housing that is destroyed. Thus far, the CHA Plan for Transformation has destroyed approximately 7,738 public housing apartments. The neighborhoods themselves are slated for gentrification with the goal of public housing projects replaced by mixed-income neighborhoods that offer a modicum of affordable housing but a whole lot of market-rate condos and town houses for urban professionals. Consequently, large numbers of recipients of public housing are displaced to other communities, to homelessness, or to the suburbs, which are developing pockets of extreme poverty. Rich whites are taking back the city center following decades of white flight and planned isolation for the high-rise projects corralled by highways. What appears in Chicago is a partial reversal of 1950s white flight and suburbanization. Certain suburbs are more exclusive than ever, while others are becoming enclaves of poverty. As the city gets more and more gentrified, the people who work the minimum-wage jobs downtown are traveling hours a day on public transportation to get to work. Those with the least control over their time have their time further squeezed. This is different from the long commutes faced by suburban salaried workers whose time commitment is rewarded with potential economic and career opportunity as well as public schools receiving high public investment. In fact, the gentrification of neighborhoods and the dismantling of public housing are now being reported in the popular press as resulting in poverty and gang activity in the suburbs.[28]

To make matters worse, real estate developers and the numerous law firms involved in these public-private partnerships are receiving truly massive subsidies from federal and city public money that could otherwise directly provide public housing assistance. What is being justified on the grounds of the inherent efficiencies of the market against the inherent inefficiencies of the public sectors appears a lot like the skimming of public money. At the same time, governance over public planning is increasingly shifted to real estate developers who have financial incentives to put draconian restrictions on the affordable housing residents in the new mixed-income developments. Developers want to draw the 80 percent middle-class and professional–class, largely white, market-rate residents by assuring them that the 20 percent working poor and largely nonwhite affordable housing recipients in the new development are not a threat. For example, developers are restricting public housing from former public housing residents with a criminal record—sometimes even restricting anyone with an extended family member with a record. These restrictions are permitted by HUD but are far more restrictive and punitive than HUD would require. Public housing governance has been shifted to the private sector and specifically to the developers who have financial stakes in the restrictions. In this case, public housing is being denied to those most in need of support. As Susan J. Popkin and Mary K. Cunningham of the Urban Institute write, "Public housing—particularly distressed public housing like the CHA's developments—served as the housing of last resort for America's poorest for decades. A substantial proportion of those still living in these distressed developments are literally one step away from becoming homeless—and may become so if they are relocated to the private market."[29]

There are a number of false assumptions undergirding these public-private partnerships:

- Public housing through direct provision inevitably results in compounded problems and concentrated poverty; therefore, public-private partnerships must be better.
- If market and private developers are involved in public housing, the efficiencies of the market will necessarily benefit housing recipients.

- The private sector is always more efficient than the public sector, so these privatizations must be a step in the right direction.

Although Chicago's public housing projects did showcase some of the worst aspects of failed urban planning, this history of failure to invest in public services does not mean that market-based solutions are the only way for publicly funded housing to be directly provided, inexpensive, and highly accessible. Perhaps the least convincing argument for privatization of public housing is the one about financial efficiencies. The move to privatization has introduced a system that takes public housing funding and uses the vast majority to finance market-rate housing and private developer profit. The myth of the market as always more efficient manages to hang on to the popular imagination despite such gross inefficiencies as Iraq contracting, Wall Street scandals from Enron to HealthSouth, and the need for a number of entire industries to remain reliant on the public sector to remain financially viable, including the airlines, insurance, agriculture, high tech, and defense. Never mind the inefficiencies of corporate culture that would be obvious to anyone who has ever been to a big-box store or tried to use an electronic switchboard system to get information from, say, a cable company. What the city and business groups is touting as efficiencies and urban renewal is a combination of real estate profiteering and land grabs at the expense of the most vulnerable. These projects offer public support and security for investors while undermining support and security for the poorest.

The Gentrification Link between Housing and School Privatization

In the winter of 2005, I attended a downtown forum hosted by the Metropolitan Planning Council. This forum brought together corporate professionals with city and public school officials, such as Chicago Public Schools CEO Arne Duncan; the superintendent of the Portland, Oregon, public schools; and a leader of Renaissance 2010 at the University of Chicago. In the panelists' talks, business rhetoric was ceaselessly invoked to claim Renaissance 2010 and other programs like it in Boston and Portland were going to result in "high achievement" through injecting a healthy dose of "competition" and "choice," and how charter schools "free from bureaucratic constraints" would have the authority to do the right thing.

I was hardly surprised by this rhetoric as it now dominates policy and popular school reform literature. What did surprise me slightly was the booming silence about the displacement of community members from their neighborhoods. Equally astonishing was the refusal to acknowledge how changes in economic class and racial/ethnic composition that result from gentrification bear on test-based achievement gains. Participants spoke of the increases they expected in standardized tests as vindication for the plan to dismantle public schools and put in place charter schools. No one acknowledged how standardized tests affirm and reward the knowledge of students of class, race, and ethnic privilege while disaffirming the knowledge of minority students. So as Renaissance 2010 results in a higher proportion of privileged students in any given school by reopening schools in newly gentrified neighborhoods, the predictable result will be higher test scores. But this is hardly a triumph for those who lived in the community before who can no longer attend the schools, because the schools are selective enrollment, or because their family was forced to move out of the community for available housing, or because their family was made homeless by the dismantling of their public housing and the closing of their public school.

Proponents for Renaissance 2010 use the ideal of small schools to suggest that the newly opened schools will benefit from this change of form. As Michael Klonsky and William Ayers, two Chicago-based leaders of the small schools movement and opponents of Renaissance 2010, write, the original goal of the small schools movement was community-based democratic education. They point out that Renaissance 2010 privileges charters run by EMOs like The Edison Schools.[30] In their view, the small schools movement has been co-opted by the business sector and reduced to a cliché as the social justice dimensions have been dropped in favor of a neoliberal vision for market fundamentalism.

> Even before it got off the ground, Ren 10 was being hailed as a "reform model" for other large urban districts. It looms as part of a new national wave of fierce market fundamentalism, now being touted as the ownership society, with ownership supposedly the common national goal shared by Enron executives, factory workers, and public housing residents alike. It's apparent everywhere these days, penetrating our schools, homes, families, places of worship—even our private lives. The "ownership society," in matters of public policy, is a narrowly reimagined and redefined public space, cannibalizing everything from health care to retirement benefits, criminal justice, waste management, elections, public safety, and water rights. Any area that has traditionally been part of the common good and publicly administered is now up for grabs, and public schools are no exception. Public space is being divided into sectors to be sold off or privately managed.[31]

Ayers and Klonsky's point importantly highlights the relationships between the roles schools play in fostering particular kinds of subjectivities and the broader social and individual visions animating social policy and school reform. Renaissance 2010 is imagined as a singular accommodationist reform within which students are to learn what is determined from above as important to learn so that they can "achieve" academically. Then, ideally, this school achievement can be cashed in for work opportunities in the corporate-controlled economy later. This contrasts starkly with the democratic education ideals that seek to teach students to understand and theorize the problems facing their community that they experience so as to act with others to transform those conditions. Such community-based democratic educational practices need to be guided by overarching democratic principles. Democratic principles need to emphasize the relationships between claims to knowledge and political control, economic control, and cultural control. Corporate educational reforms such as Renaissance 2010 and NCLB evacuate politics, reducing educational practice to the alleged neutral and objective singularity of the attainment of knowledge claimed to be universally valuable. This false neutrality and objectivity conceals the relationships between knowledge and authority and deceptively installs class-based knowledge as universally valuable. The people who own the means of production assimilate everyone to their interests by making it seem to the working classes that their interests are the same. So you get the idea, for instance, that the freedom to shop is as good for me as a citizen as it is for the people who are profiting from my shopping. Standardized testing and standardization of curriculum are some of the most effective tools in schools for disguising the erasure of class from the making and organization of knowledge.[32] Particularly at a historical moment of radically worsening inequalities in wealth and income, this process is decidedly at odds with democratic ideals of equality and justice.

The "ownership society" ideal undergirding Renaissance 2010 and pushed by the political Right suggests that individuals need to think of themselves as entrepreneurs who are principally and ultimately *individually* responsible for their own well-being in society. This view has a certain appeal in its invocation of individual freedom understood through self-reliance. To be enterprising, creative, and self-reliant are widely appealing individual values across the political spectrum with deep historical resonances. However, when such individual ideals are put forward as social ideals and social policy, they conceal the differences between the individual and the social. For example, even the most enterprising, creative, and self-reliant person does not act in a vacuum.

Rather, the intelligibility of individual interpretations and creative acts is socially dependent. The choices individuals make are bound by social contexts. Very few, if any, enterprises that individuals seek to achieve have value or meaning apart from the social world. And the decisions people make impact not only themselves but society. The "ownership society" ideal behind Renaissance 2010 suggests shifting social responsibility for the public good onto individuals. What is at stake here is not the ideal of radical individualism versus the ideal of collectivism because the kind of pure radical individualism idealized by the term *ownership society* is an ideology or myth. Rather, "ownership society" projects such as Renaissance 2010 do not shift social policy governance and social responsibility onto individuals. They shift governance onto those with more social and political power on the false justification that this gives individuals greater freedom and choice. In the case of Renaissance 2010, decision-making power over which schools to close and which to open, which teachers to retain, hire, and fire, whose curriculum to teach, who attends the schools, who has oversight—all of these get shifted to business groups and the politicians they back and away from the broader public—community members, parents, teachers, and students. In this case entrepreneurialism seems to apply most to those seeking to start a for-profit or nonprofit school. However, the application process for starting a school approximates a command economy more than it does the free market.

Recall McKenna's statement: "No other major city has launched such an ambitious public school choice agenda." In practice, the rhetoric of "choice" as it pertains to Renaissance 2010 is dishonest as many of the new schools are not open enrollment but rather are selective enrollment or lottery based. The children who live in the community may not have the opportunity to attend the new Renaissance school in their neighborhood. I saw this firsthand in my Edgewater neighborhood as one of the new Renaissance schools was a JROTC naval academy. The military academy was stuffed into the already-existing school, Senn High School, which had served a diverse, multicultural, largely immigrant student body.

This move highlighted the disingenuousness of proponents of Renaissance 2010 who claim that it improves educational quality by making smaller schools with less overcrowding. What was done to Senn was the opposite—producing overcrowding. Under the plan the school lost a third of its physical space, and the best-equipped and -maintained parts of the school were taken and given to the selective enrollment military academy. This cherry-picking of public school resources typifies how Renaissance 2010 generally pillages public schooling to bolster the experimental and private models rather than to strengthen public schools.[33]

In 2004, I attended meetings and rallies against the Senn plan and witnessed vast community opposition. Despite the committed activism of a number of organizations such as the Save Senn Coalition, Andersonville Neighbors for Peace, Teachers for Social Justice, and other groups, the city and Chicago Public Schools ignored the choices of the community, ignored the choices of the vast majority of the student body of the school, ignored the choices of the teachers in the school. At one heated event at the school, the Chicago Public Schools representatives and a military officer arrived with the intention of propagandizing the value of the military academy by showing a video. The representatives refused a dialogue about the plan and insisted that the community be a passive audience. Roughly one thousand irate community members, parents, teachers, and students refused to watch the video, repeatedly booing it off the screen. Officials stormed out as participants pleaded with them to stay and engage in debate over the plan.

The event became a public community forum in which students, teachers, parents, and community members voiced their opposition to the plan. Teachers quickly organized translators as testimony was translated into several languages. The arguments were videotaped and later aired on public-access television. Speakers that night criticized not just Renaissance 2010 and the military academy. Most linked these local issues to broader political matters, pointing out how the military academy targets poor and nonwhite youth for recruitment to fight poor and nonwhite people in the war in Iraq. Some teachers harshly criticized the military curriculum as being at odds with the values of schooling in a democratic society. Students pointed out that the school's culture that respects diversity is threatened by the antigay position of the military. The public deliberation that formed in opposition typified some of the best aspects of what public schooling can facilitate in a democracy—the event fostered the linking of struggles over knowledge to broader political, ethical, and economic questions. The installation of the Rickover Academy at Senn signifies the ways that Renaissance 2010 ignores both community and individual choice while aiming to destroy public democratic educational possibilities.[34]

As Lipman suggests in referring to plans to close Englewood High School on the South Side, "The closing of schools is linked concretely and symbolically to the destruction of the communities."[35]

New Disasters: The Corporate Takeover of Chicago Schools and Communities

As the previously cited quote by the Commercial Club's Andrew McKenna attests, Renaissance 2010 is a privatization plan. The new schools are charter schools, contract schools, and performance schools. Calling them "contract schools" appears to be a creative way for the city to circumvent the state limit on the number of charter schools. They allow outside operators to run the schools. Two-thirds of the schools will be nonunion. In the second round of school selection, sixteen bids out of sixteen went to nonunion EMOs, including William Bennett's largely discredited K12, which sells conservative curriculum online to charter schools and homeschoolers.[36]

The Commercial Club of Chicago, in conjunction with the Chicago Public Education Fund, established the New Schools for Chicago organization (NSC). The Commercial Club pledged to raise about $25 million from the corporate sector for NSC, which it will use to support financially and technically the closing and reopening of public schools in their new form. This plan is crucially about shifting public school governance under the more complete direction of the business sector and away from control by teachers, teachers unions, and community residents. Harrison Steans, chair of Financial Investments Corp. and chair of the Education Committee of the Civic Committee of the Commercial Club, described NSC as "probably the most important long-term project the Civic Committee has ever undertaken. Its strength lies in the partnership between Mayor Daley, the Chicago Public Schools and the business and philanthropic communities."[37] Lipman writes that NSC is "comprised of several of the Commercial Club's corporate CEOs along with CPS leaders. This 'shadow cabinet,' as it was dubbed in a *Chicago Sun-Times* article in November 2004, includes the chairs of McDonald's Corporation and Northern Trust Bank, a partner in a leading corporate law firm, the retired chair of the Tribune Corporation, and the CEO of the Chicago Community Trust—a major corporate foundation. It has the power to recommend new school operators and evaluate the schools."[38]

According to the president of the Civic Committee, R. Eden Martin, the plan will result in high quality and high achievement because school choice will foster competition between schools. "We believe the New Schools for Chicago will provide families with educational options and create a more competitive environment—which will lead to higher academic standards and greater accountability in all public schools."[39] This clichéd string of business metaphors has been invoked ceaselessly for the last decade to justify charter

schools, voucher schemes, and the subversion of democratically elected school boards.

The logic is frankly outlandish. The idea is that in order
to improve the quality of public schooling, what is necessary is first cutting back on public funding. This makes no
sense considering that the best public schooling has the
highest levels of public investments. The second premise is
that schools should be made to compete against each other
for scarce resources. This makes no sense because some
schools will necessarily lose out to other schools, and the
playing field for such competition is already skewed from the
outset by historical inequalities in funding, the demographic
composition of the student body, and the different levels of
cultural capital students and teachers have in the different
schools. This has been done already to no good effect in
Chicago through Paul Vallas's destructive "reconstitution"
of Chicago Public Schools that first threatens and then punishes those schools that don't make numerically quantifiable
"achievement" gains determined by tests. Reconstitution also
failed in San Francisco.[40] The third premise is that "just like in
business" (which is not at all what happens in real business),
when schools—with their resources cut and their workers
put under extreme pressure—do not improve, they should
be allowed to "go out of business." This makes no sense in
principle because public schools have a *public* mission of
universal public education rather than a private mission of
accumulation of profit. It makes no sense in practice as the
experiments in public schools being run like businesses
(EMOs) or being deregulated (charter schools) do not show
any evidence of being in any way better than public schooling. In fact, there is plenty of evidence of multiple deficits,
from financial problems to oversight problems and testing
scandals.[41]

Deb Moore, editor of the journal *School Planning and
Management,* confuses the business takeover of school plan-
ning from the community as citizen involvement, writing,
"I applaud the citizens of Chicago for taking responsibility

and becoming active participants in the education of their students!" Moore actually has it backward, as the citizens of the communities in question have come out in force to resist and protest Renaissance 2010. Rather than bringing citizens of communities into the planning of public schooling, as Ayers and Klonsky suggest, Renaissance 2010 favors politically connected private firms, and management and efficiency plans over democratic governance.[42]

One central way that Renaissance 2010 shifts governance is by undermining or dismantling democratically elected local school councils (LSCs), which were established in 1988. These councils involve parents, teachers, and community members in overseeing and planning the running of public schools with principals. LSCs made Chicago a national model for decentralized school governance and allowed the community to govern finances and hire principals.[43] Under Renaissance 2010, not only are these bypassed, but the new schools will have appointed transitional advisory councils (TACs). According to Lipman, "they are a means for the Board of Education to advance its agenda without serious community input but nevertheless give the impression of community involvement."[44] Although the Renaissance 2010 Web site claims that TACs represent a wide array of citizens, critics contend that they are dominated by businesspeople and politicians. Ultimately, they serve an advisory role, thereby abetting the shift of decision-making power upward to Chicago Public Schools.

Proponents of Renaissance 2010 contend that the plan gives greater autonomy to schools, thereby allowing a greater diversity of school models and experimentation. As Ayers and Klonsky point out, however, "The EMOs use the language of autonomy to evade community engagement and collective bargaining with teachers. . . . We worry that 'autonomy' can become another business code word signaling management's freedom to do whatever it chooses at the expense of teachers and communities."[45] As Renaissance 2010 is so thoroughly dominated by business planning, the possibilities for a wide range of alternative democratic and progressive models to be developed are likely to be highly contained.

What is more, with the heavy reliance of charter schools on philanthropic support for operations, the school models will need to cohere with the dominant trends of the moment, such as quality and achievement defined narrowly through standardized curriculum and standardized testing. Thus, the organizational structure will tend toward the diminishment of autonomy. Moreover, any charter and contract schools run by for-profit companies like The Edison Schools will need to make up for the resources being skimmed for investor profits and will be yet more dependent on business-oriented philanthropies and narrow definitions of school quality and legitimacy.

The wide-scale privatization fostered by Renaissance 2010 radically shifts governance in the name of increased "accountability." Yet, Lewis Cohen wisely insists that "while these management systems—whether in medicine or in education—are imposed in the name of accountability, the question of accountability to whom is rarely dissected. In the case of managed care, it is accountability to shareholders and the bottom line that supersedes patient needs. Likewise, private managers of schools meet the needs of students, families, and communities only to the extent that doing so improves their bottom line."[46]

Resistance

Though public governance is being robbed by Renaissance 2010, the public is fighting back. The Chicago Teachers Union collected fifteen thousand signatures on a petition against Renaissance 2010, and the president of the union has pointed out just how poorly Chicago charter schools have performed according to the test-based measures that proponents of the plan care about. In November 2004, a thousand Chicagoans rallied at the Thompson Center downtown, where CTU president Marilyn Stewart spoke:

Chapter 3

"Renaissance 2010 is an untested and rushed initiative that will create the displacement of 20,000 students and the loss of employment for thousands of union workers."[47] The union has pledged to work with a wide coalition of activists and organizations. Ayers and Klonsky point to growing resistance to Renaissance 2010, including revolt by some of the TACs. But they remind readers that in many cases the community's will has been trampled.[48]

For citizens organizing against Renaissance 2010, the linkage between school reform and land grab by business is at the center. Lipman recounts a meeting in February 2005 in the targeted African American Englewood neighborhood. "Parents, students, and teachers described the history of disinvestment in their schools and community and argued that Renaissance 2010 is driving gentrification and removal of low-income African Americans. 'We're being pushed out of the city under the guise of school reform,' one speaker said."[49]

The corporatization of public schooling in Chicago through both Renaissance 2010 and No Child Left Behind ought to be understood in relation to what is being done in the wake of Hurricane Katrina and the war in Iraq. Public infrastructure is being grabbed by business interests, and public governance is being usurped. This is facilitated in part by business ideology that misrepresents the public interest in private terms. What is necessary to combat this is not only activism but also critical pedagogical projects that can cut through business propaganda and teach students, parents, and teachers to analyze claims made by privatizers. Beyond contesting propaganda, if public schooling stands any chance of developing as a site for the production of democratic culture, then those committed to challenging these destructive politics can learn to turn acts of interpretation into acts of political intervention. This involves interrogating claims to knowledge in terms of the material interests and the assumptions undergirding claims to truth, developing capacities to comprehend how meaning-making practices are involved in producing identifications and identities, and linking up such interpretive questions to both broader structures of power and courses of concrete action to change them. Democratic culture is not fixed and stable. Nor is it imposed on people from above. Democratic culture is a process, and it is continually struggled over. While privatizing public schools threatens to reduce the places that foster democratic culture, the struggle itself for democratic culture cannot be smashed, and no one can take it from the people.

Notes

1. Details on Oakwood Shores can be found at the Web site of the Community Builders, Inc.—http://www.tcbinc.org/who_we_are/wwa_overview.htm—as well as the Web site of the Hyde Park-Kenwood Community Conference: http://www.hydepark.org/education/UCschools.htm. Oakwood Shores has two different Web sites, one for the public housing (http://www.oakwoodshores.com) and one for the expensive market-rate housing (http://www.thearchesatoakwoodshores.com).

2. See http://www.oakwoodshores.com.

3. Community Builders, http://www.tcbinc.org/who_we_are/wwa_overview.htm.

4. View the public housing application requirements at http://www.oakwoodshores.com.

5. Kate N. Grossman, "From Eyesores to Oakwood Shores," *Chicago Sun-Times,* June 14, 2006, available at http://www.suntimes.com.

6. See the CHA Plan for Transformation Web site: http://www.thecha.org/transformplan/files/fy2005_mtw_appendices.pdf.

7. Community Builders, http://www.tcbinc.org/who_we_are/wwa_overview.htm.

8. Pauline Lipman, "'We're Not Blind. Just Follow the Dollar Sign,'" *Rethinking Schools Online* 19, no. 4 (Summer 2005), available at http://www.rethinkingschools.org. Though the University of Chicago Charter School is a nonprofit charter, most of the new charters being opened through Renaissance 2010 are in fact for profit. However, nonprofit charters participate in the broader

privatization agenda by weakening investment in universal public schooling, threatening teachers unions, and weakening teacher certification requirements.

9. George Clowes, "Competition and Partnerships Are Key to Renaissance Plan," *Heartland Institute,* October 1, 2004, available at http://www.heartland.org.

10. Available at the A. T. Kearney's Web site: http://www. atkearney.com.

11. Edward Wiley, William Mathis, and David Garcia, "The Impact of the Adequate Yearly Progress Requirement of the Federal 'No Child Left Behind' Act on Schools in the Great Lakes Region," *Educational Policy Studies Laboratory,* September 2005, p. 3 of "Executive Summary," available at http://edpolicylab.org.

12. Wiley et al., "The Impact of the Adequate Yearly Progress Requirement."

13. See, for example, the contributors in Deborah Meier and George Wood, eds., *Many Children Left Behind* (Boston: Beacon, 2004). Also see, for example, the writing of Stan Karp ("Taming the Beast," *Rethinking Schools* 18, no. 4 [Summer 2004]; "Bandaids or Bulldozers," *Rethinking Schools* 20, no. 3 [Spring 2006]; and "The No Child Left Behind Hoax," http://www.rethinkingschools. org/special_reports/bushplan/hoax.shtml) and Gerald Bracey (in addition to his recent books like *Setting the Record Straight: Responses to Misconceptions about Public Education in the United States* [Alexandria, Va.: Association for Supervision and Curriculum Development, 1997], his blogs on the Huffington Post [www. huffingtonpost.com] provide insightful commentary) on NCLB. A number of excellent resources on privatization and commercialism implications of NCLB can be found at the site of the Educational Policy Studies Laboratory at http://www.schoolcommercialism. org. More critical and theoretical approaches to NCLB that situate it in relation to broader economic and cultural forces can be found in the *Journal of Critical Educational Policy Studies* and *Policy Futures in Education.* See the excellent work of David Hursh on NCLB, such as Hursh and Camille Anne Martina, "Neoliberalism and Schooling in the U.S.: How State and Federal Government Education Policies Perpetuate Inequality," *Journal for Critical Educational Policy Studies* 1, no. 2 (October 2003).

14. Jonathan Kozol, *The Shame of a Nation: The Restoration of Apartheid Schooling in America* (New York: Crown, 2005).

15. Alfie Kohn, "NCLB and the Effort to Privatize Public Education," in Many *Children Left Behind,* ed. Meier and Wood, 79–100.

16. Sharon L. Nichols, Gene V. Glass, and David C. Berliner, "High-Stakes Testing and Student Achievement: Problems for the No Child Left Behind Act," Educational Policy Studies Laboratory, p. 3 of "Executive Summary," available at http://edpolicylab.org.

17. Deb Moore, "A New Approach in Chicago," *School Planning and Management,* July 2004, 8.

18. "Snapshot: Chicago Renaissance 2010," 2, Bill and Melinda Gates Foundation, http://www.gatesfoundation.org/Education/RelatedInfo/Possibilities/Possibilities2004.

19. Lipman, "'We're Not Blind.'"

20. Dorothy Shipps, *School Reform, Corporate Style: Chicago 1880–2000* (Lawrence: University of Kansas Press, 2006), x.

21. Shipps's question raises another matter that has been largely ignored in public discourse and educational policy: how is it that the corporate sector and the government are able to represent business as a savior for public schooling when they have been getting bad grades for a century? One answer is corporate media, the most powerful producer of knowledge about public schooling.

22. Pauline Lipman, "TSJ Critique of Renaissance 2010 Statement to the Board of Education by Pauline Lipman August 25, 2004," *Substance,* December 2004, available at http://www.substancenews.com.

23. Christopher Manning, "African Americans," *Encyclopedia of Chicago,* http://www.encyclopedia.chicagohistory.org/pages/27.html.

24. Jonathan Kozol, *Savage Inequalities: Children in America's Schools* (New York: HarperPerennial, 1992).

25. William Ayers and Michael Klonsky, "Chicago's Renaissance 2010: The Small Schools Movement Meets the Ownership Society," *Phi Delta Kappan,* February 2006, 456.

26. Lipman, "'We're Not Blind.'"

27. Metropolitan Planning Council, "CHA Plan for Transformation," Progress Report, January 2005, available at http://www.metroplanning.org.

28. Cheryl Corely, "Report: Chicago Gang Activity Spreading to Suburbs," National Public Radio, *Morning Edition,* June 20,

2006; Sylvia Gomez, "Gangs on the Move and Headed to Suburbs," CBS2 Chicago Broadcast, June 19, 2006. The media coverage was prompted by the publication of the *Gang Book* by the Chicago Crime Commission. The book explains that gangs are being driven to the suburbs in part by the tearing down of the public housing projects and the gentrification of poor parts of the city.

29. Susan J. Popkin and Mary K. Cunningham, "Beyond the Projects: Lessons from Public Housing Transformation in Chicago," in *The Geography of Opportunity: Race and Housing Choice in Metropolitan America,* ed. Xavier de Souza Briggs (Washington, D.C.: Brookings Institution Press, 2005), 194.

30. Ayers and Klonsky, "Chicago's Renaissance 2010," 455.

31. Ayers and Klonsky, "Chicago's Renaissance 2010," 454.

32. This has been elaborately established by Pierre Bourdieu and Jean-Claude Passeron, *Reproduction in Education, Society, and Culture* (London: Sage, 1977).

33. Ayers and Klonsky, "Chicago's Renaissance 2010," 456.

34. Chicago leads the nation in developing public schools as military academies under Renaissance 2010. This points to an additional aspect of the relationship between schooling and the new politics of disaster as the most economically and politically marginalized students in the United States are primed to fight on behalf of the nation's upcoming imperial adventures, such as the market-driven destruction of Iraq. Participation is sold to students through jingoistic patriotism, promises of economic opportunity following military service, masculinism, and high-technology fun and adventure. The military academies are pushed by the city as providing students with "discipline" that they are alleged to lack—discipline that will supposedly serve them in the workplace.

35. Lipman, "'We're Not Blind.'"

36. See the report on K12 by Susan Ohanian, "The K12 Virtual Primary School History Curriculum: A Participant's-Eye View," Educational Policy Studies Laboratory at Arizona State University, http://www.asu.edu/educ/epsl/EPRU/documents/EPSL-0404-117-EPRU.doc.

37. Moore, "A New Approach in Chicago," 8.

38. Lipman, "'We're Not Blind.'"

39. Moore, "A New Approach in Chicago," 8.

40. Catherine Gewertz, "Chicago to Start Over with 100 Small Schools," *Education Week,* July 14, 2004, 1.

41. See Kenneth Saltman, *The Edison Schools: Corporate Schooling and the Assault on Public Education* (New York: Routledge, 2005).

42. Ayers and Klonsky, "Chicago's Renaissance 2010," 455.

43. Gewertz, "Chicago to Start Over," 1.

44. Jackson Potter, "Englewood High School Becomes 'Urban Prep,'" *Substance,* February–March 2006, http://www.substancenews.com/content/view/389/81.

45. William Ayers and Michael Klonsky, "Private Management of Chicago Schools Is a Long Way from Mecca," *Phi Delta Kappan,* February 2006, 462.

46. Lewis Cohen, "It's Not about Management," *Phi Delta Kappan,* February 2006, 460.

47. Anonymous, "Chicagoans Mobilize against Renaissance 2010," *American Teacher* 89, no. 6 (March 2005): 6.

48. Ayers and Klonsky, "Chicago's Renaissance 2010," 456.

49. Lipman, "'We're Not Blind.'"

CONCLUSION
From Dispossession
to Possession

Making Educational Facts on the Ground

᠊ᢒ

The preceding chapters illustrate how the educational privatization movement is taking an insidious turn toward capitalizing on disaster to achieve otherwise politically and economically failed reforms. There are two ways of thinking about this process.

The first presumes that the new assaults on public schooling are occurring because of a vast culture of corruption that has crept beyond the government scandals of the Bush administration and numerous corporate scandals to infect the field of education. Within this view, the reason for corruption is that the privatizers have failed politically, and now they are using unpolitical means to achieve these ends. What would be necessary, then, is to eradicate such corruption in order to restore the political field within which reforms can be publicly debated and deliberated over.

From these premises it is certainly possible to conceive a number of practical reforms to stem the tide of corporate profiteering in public education with the aim of restoring school reform debates to politics:

- Regulate the influence peddling of right-wing educational think tanks (Hoover, Heritage, Urban Institute, Heartland, Manhattan, Fordham, etc.) and the close ties they have to the for-profit education industry.

- Close the revolving door between government and the private sector (exemplified by Ridge, Roberti, Javdan, CAII, Horblitt, etc.).
- Control the influence of business groups on urban policy (Metropolitan Planning Council, Business Roundtable, Commercial Club, etc.).
- Disallow authoritarian seizures of school systems by governors and mayors (Pennsylvania, Illinois, Maryland, District of Columbia, Louisiana).
- Dismantle No Child Left Behind or the aspects of it that support vouchers, charters, and punitive high-stakes assessment schemes designed to dismantle schools (which are most of it).
- Implement a federal ban on advertising and marketing in public schools, and reallocate federal funds currently used to support privatization schemes toward rewarding schools for keeping public schools public.
- Support public schooling financially, and delink school funding from property taxes by following the rest of the world and equally dividing public school funding federally.

We might add:

- Refrain from illegally invading other nations and then implementing market experiments in multiple sectors, including education.

Such reforms, along with many others (e.g., electoral reform, expansive welfare state protections), might contribute to fostering the conditions within which education can provide the means for citizens to engage publicly in debate and deliberation toward the ends of self-governance. This would be the progressive dream—one that has become increasingly framed as untenable, impossible, and outdated as the logic of the market has overtaken public discourse, as neoliberal economic, political, and cultural assumptions continue to eclipse democratic ones.

The second approach to the problems detailed here takes a broader, more systemic and structural view. This is an approach that offers crucial insights yet tends to reduce the political and cultural questions at stake here to strictly economic ones. In the broader view, neoliberal privatization and deregulation—as well as "accumulation by dispossession," the pillaging of the public sphere—are manifestations of an economic system designed for continual growth—that is, the ongoing expansion of capital accumulation at any cost. In this second view, all of the reforms described here should still be done, but they would be insufficient to deal with the underlying problem of schooling in capitalism that functions largely to teach skills and know-how in ways ideologically compatible with social relations of capital accumulation. In this second view, the fundamental disaster for schooling is capitalism itself, which structures schooling in both form and content in ways incompatible with democratic dispositions of questioning, criticism, defiance of authoritarianism, collective enactment of public priorities, dialogue, embrace of fallibilism, and eschewing of dogma. Like capitalist mass media, capitalist schooling tends to produce passivity and spectatorship, as well as to undermine political agency, while producing frameworks of interpretation compatible with the hierarchical and inegalitarian tendencies of capitalism, including the production of cultural difference in unequal forms that foster capital accumulation.[1] (This is aside from the other megadisasters accruing from capitalism, including vast environmental destruction that could result in environmental collapse and politically driven disaster that could result in nuclear annihilation).

There are two crucial points to be made here about economics and politics in this broader systemic view. The first is that capitalism is not merely an economic system; it is also a political system organizing social relations in hierarchical ways while subordinating the interests of people and the public to the accumulation of capital. Such a political configuration is utterly incompatible with democracy. Any notion of education that aspires to foster a democratic society must opt for economic arrangements commensurate with democracy and educational practices that enact a vision for democracy. All dominant educational reform trends presently move in the opposite direction, subjugating the making of a free-thinking critical citizenry to the imperatives of capital. What is more, it is specifically those parts of public education that are redundant to processes of economic reproduction that are being targeted for privatization. The obvious example is the targeting of the poorest public schools for multiple forms of privatization. The students in poor and working-class schools are being largely warehoused and prepared for economic exclusion or interchangeable and disposable wage labor. However, these students are made into economically productive forces by being socialized for submission to wage labor in the service economy, commodified as prisoners for the prison-industrial complex, or made into soldiers who will participate in expropriating the resources of other nations. On rare occasions, they can transcend class lines and be professionals. Public school privatization makes disposable students into an *immediate* investment opportunity. Students in privileged public schools serve as a *deferred* investment as they largely produce leaders and professionals who will play crucial and rarer, less interchangeable roles in reproducing the economy. Put differently, students in working-class and poor schools are being produced as nonproductive forces, part of a growing disposable population of citizens.[2] In this case, what I have detailed in New Orleans, Iraq, Chicago, and around the United States under NCLB reveals intensified efforts to capitalize on students.

Students in working-class and poor public schools within the perspective of a capitalist economy have little value beyond their roles as consumers, providers of cheap labor, or units to be commodified for privatization schemes. However, from the perspective of democratic political ideals, these students have value as citizens and human beings who can become decisive democratic forces in the political arena. This relates closely to the second point.

Second, education has truly radical possibilities for social transformation. Oppressive and exclusionary economic and political systems can only be sustained by a public that has accepted its basic terms and assumptions—that is, a public that has accepted a culture of domination, a culture that succeeds in making subjects who understand themselves through oppressive values and identifications. In other words, the social formation can only be sustained and reproduced by the ongoing education of subjects with the values and beliefs conducive to the maintenance of power relations. New pedagogical practices produce not only new knowledge, values, and identifications. A truly critical education dedicated to the ruthless interrogation of truths, their making, whose interests they serve, and what kinds of identities they form can provide the intellectual tools to imagine and enact a different future from the one prescribed by the dictates of corporate profit and state actions to assist it. Public schools continue to be a crucial site and stake of struggle for a radically democratic society.

Since my focus here is on the ways that educational privatization is part of the broader movement through which public resources are being pillaged for capital accumulation, I want to borrow a term from the ongoing colonial legacy of dispossessive power.

The founders of Israel spoke of making "facts on the ground." This term refers to shaping material reality in ways that institutionalize and make solid that which is, in fact, a recent innovation. For example, Israel eradicated Palestinian towns, removing all traces, all physical markers from which public memory of the history of the place could be conjured, invoked, or referenced. On this land Israel then made monuments to martyred soldiers, built towns, and made facts on the ground. Such material production creates institutional and public memory while also working to conceal that which was there before. The longer it takes to rebuild schools and communities in New Orleans, the more powerful that wreckage becomes as new facts on the ground. The longer residents are kept from returning, the easier it becomes to represent the land as being an open frontier, the colonial dream of open space to be settled by real estate developers with the help of the government. The longer the charter school network and voucher scheme function, the more they become facts on the ground. The longer they become facts on the ground, the harder it becomes to remember what was there before: the teachers union, the collective bargaining agreements, the democratically elected school board, the public control. Not only does it become harder to remember what was lost, but it becomes less imaginable to conceive of building on what was there before. How can you build on what is not there?

This may sound despairing, but I am going to propose something radically hopeful: that conceiving of facts on the ground opens up a new way of thinking about the struggle for democratic public education as part of a broader struggle for critical democracy. What would it mean to create new facts on the ground, democratic facts on the ground that function as public pedagogy and create new horizons of possibility for future action?

Action creates a different context and hence new possibilities for future action.[3] Three clear examples of this from radically different political perspectives are the invasion of Iraq, the terrorist attacks of September 11, 2001, and the worker takings of bankrupt factories in Argentina following the collapse of the economy under neoliberal governance.[4] In the case of the invasion of Iraq, the neoconservatives derided what they referred to as the "reality-based community" for failing to grasp that by invading, they changed the event horizon for future possible actions. In other words, aside from the fact that the invasion was monstrous, murderous, wrong, illegal, unethical (and it was, and it should not have been done), the invasion changed what was possible to think and to say and to do. Once done, certain avenues that were open before are now foreclosed. New avenues are possible (not necessarily good ones or better ones—in fact, certainly worse). Likewise, the attacks of 9/11 did not just change the physical landscape; they changed what was imaginable, and they opened up a struggle over the memory and meaning of that place. The taking of factories by workers in Argentina following the financial collapse resulted in not simply the making of collectively owned and managed industry with mutually supporting businesses. It also expanded what was imaginable for the rest of the economy and expanded what could be imagined for other places and nations with moribund industries. In seizing the factories and making egalitarian, fair, and collectively determined processes and priorities, in instituting economic democracy, the workers made facts on the ground. Public schools must also be taken back by the public, for the public.

The political Right is moving to dispossess the public of its homes and schools in order to profit. Public schools belong to the public. Public housing belongs to the public. Public parks belong to the public. Even the military is bound to defend the Constitution and belongs to the public. What would it mean to materially repossess public goods? What would it mean to make facts on the ground, to make educational institutions?

Such a project of making educational facts on the ground can begin by working hegemonically through already-existing institutions. The first question is, What are the many ways that democratic cultural politics can be fostered within public schools to reinvigorate democratic culture everywhere? There is already an enormous defensive backlash against such anticritical movements as the standardization of curriculum and the high-stakes testing regime. But progressives need to take the offensive by putting forward critical curriculum and approaches. For example, in one high school project in Los Angeles, teachers have developed a project for working-class and poor, predominantly African American and Latino students—students who have been designated by the school as "at risk" of academic failure. Teachers teach students to read and use critical sociology, cultural studies, and other scholarship from the humanities and social sciences to criticize and analyze community social problems and then to act to address these problems while continuing to draw on this scholarship to theorize their experiences. These teachers report spectacular academic success with these students who had been consigned to the penal conveyor belt. And while academic achievement on its own is hardly a worthwhile goal, these students develop political agency by practicing cultural politics as a part of broader political movements. An exciting collection of numerous scholar/teachers working with youth called *Beyond Resistance: Youth Activism and Community Change* offers detailed discussion of ongoing projects with similar ideals.[5] Likewise, in Porto Alegre, Brazil, citizen schools are working to integrate learning with social and material problems, drawing on the work of Paulo Freire and incorporating new media and expanding the pedagogical uses of critical media literacy. Scholars and teachers in the United States and around the world are learning about such critical pedagogical models to expand them in public schools, to remake public schools.

Critical pedagogies built of seemingly ephemeral words, dialogue, and print create new possibilities for future action and lay the foundations for radically different material realities.

Notes

1. See, for example, how this has been done historically with gender in Silvia Federici, *Caliban and the Witch: Women, the Body, and Primitive Accumulation* (New York: Autonomedia, 2004).

2. On the politics of disposability, see Zygmunt Bauman, *Wasted Lives* (New York: Polity, 2005), and Henry Giroux, *Stormy Weather* (Boulder, Colo.: Paradigm, 2006).

3. See Slavoj Ziþek, "Introduction," in V. I. Lenin, *Revolution at the Gates: A Selection of Writings from February to October 1917,* ed. Slavoj Ziþek (New York: Verso, 2002).

4. See Ari Berman and Naomi Klein's excellent documentary film *The Take* (2005).

5. Shawn Ginwright, Pedro Noguera, and Julio Cammarota, *Beyond Resistance! Youth Activism and Community Change: New Democratic Possibilities for Practice and Policy for America's Youth* (New York: Routledge, 2006).

Index

Index

Bush administration: and corruption, 42; and military, 113n14; and Millennium Challenge Account, 71; and New Orleans, 30–32, 36–37; and pedagogy, 75; and vouchers, 33
business. *See* corporations
Business Roundtable, 55

Cabrini-Green, 130, 132
CAII. *See* Creative Associates International, Incorporated
Camp Dresser & McKee, 118n73
capitalism: critique of, 157–58. *See also* disaster capitalism
Carter administration, 85
Catholic Church, 85
Catholic League, 32
Cedras, Raoul, 87
Central Intelligence Agency, 85
charter schools: in Chicago, 122–23, 125, 149n8; in Iraq, 6, 107; NCLB and, 7; in New Orleans, 33–34, 50–60; problems with, 54–55, 147
Chatterjee, Pratap, 73
Cheney, Dick, 115n30
Chertoff, Michael, 24
Chevron, 115n30
Chicago: housing privatization in, 3, 130–37; school reform in, 1, 6, 119–53
Chicago Housing Authority (CHA), 121
Chicago Public Education Fund, 144
Chicago Teachers Union, 147
Chile, 9
choice, rhetoric of, 141
choice schools, 127
Chubb, John, 9, 67n92, 117n64
civil society: in Haiti, 94; in Iraq, 73; neoconservatism and, 74–75
Clancy, Patrick, 123

Clinton administration, 113n14
Coalition Provisional Authority, 102
Cohen, Lewis, 147
Cohen, Sharon, 49, 55, 67n82
Commercial Club of Chicago, 6, 55, 125–26, 144
commercialism: recommendations for, 156; in schools, 4
commons, enclosing, 12, 78
Community Labor United, 61
Community United to Reform Education (CURE), 52
conservatism. *See* neoconservatism; right wing
contractors: in Chicago, 135–36; in New Orleans, 39–48
contract schools, 125, 143–44
Contras, 85
corporations: and charter schools, 56–60; versus citizen involvement, 145–46; and education, 10, 65n51; and eminent domain, 51–52; in Iraq, 69–118; and New Orleans, 21–68; recommendations for, 156; and Renaissance 2010, 125–26; rhetoric of, 10, 59, 129, 144–45; and vouchers, 37–38. *See also* for-profit corporations
corruption: and New Orleans rebuilding, 39–44; recommendations for, 155–56
Cowen, Scott, 58
Creative Associates International Incorporated (CAII), 2, 5–6, 69–118; characteristics of, 80–84; in Haiti, 87–99; in Iraq, 99–111; in Nicaragua, 84–87; performance of, 103–4; projects of, 70; and subcontractors, 104, 117n73
cultural pedagogy, disaster capitalism and, 14–16
Cunningham, Mary K., 136

Index

tism and, 75; recommendations for, 159-61

performance schools, 125

Picard, Cecil, 26, 52, 59

polyarchy, 109-10; definition of, 89, 112n11

Popkin, Susan J., 136

principals, charter schools and, 56-57

privatization: back door, 5-7; CAII and, 107; and charter schools, 53; in Chicago, 125, 130-37; and disaster capitalism, 1-2; effects of, 124-25; failures of, 3-4, 145; and gentrification, 137-43; goals of, 31; Harvey on, 77-78; in Iraq, 72-73; and new disasters, 120-21, 143-47; in New Orleans, 21-68; smash and grab, 7; strategies of, 5

Project Purple, 56

property taxes, 156

public good: individuals and, 141; versus markets, 31

public-private partnerships, assumptions of, 136-37

public schools: current state of, 4; and democracy, 14; financing, recommendations for, 156; functions of, in capitalist state, 12-13, 79, 110-11; militarization of, 77, 113n19, 141-43, 152n34; in New Orleans, 21-68; seizure of, in New Orleans, 48-50; vouchers and, 29

public sector, privatization of, 124

punishment, NCLB and, 127-28

PURE, 61

Quality Education Is a Civil Right, 61

racial segregation, vouchers and, 29, 35

racism: and Chicago housing privatization, 131-32, 137-43; Katrina rescue efforts and, 23-24

RAMAK, 90-96

Rastegar, Farshad, 104

Rawls, John, 141-42

Reagan, Ronald, 85

real estate: rhetoric of, 21-22. *See also* development; gentrification

rebuilding: and disaster capitalism, 1; for-profit corporations and, 41; in Iraq, 69; in New Orleans, problems of, 48-50; recommendations for, 159-60; rhetoric of, 27; teachers unions on, 33

Renaissance 2010, 1, 6, 119-53; effects of, 120; and housing, 130-37; Mid-South plan, 133-34; and NCLB, 125-30; resistance to, 139-40, 142-43, 147-49

repression, shift to, 77-78

Repressive State Apparatuses (RSAs), 76

reproduction, and accumulation, 12-13

Research Triangle Institute, 101, 117n73

resistance: in Chicago, 139-40, 142-43, 147-49; in New Orleans, 60-61; recommendations for, 155-63; resources for, 61

Revitalization of Iraqi Schools and Stabilization of Education (RISE), 101

Rex Organization, 56

rhetoric: of autonomy, 146-47; of choice, 141; of corporations, 10, 59, 129, 144-45; of neoconservatism, 71; of real estate, 21-22; of rebuilding, 27

Rice, Condoleezza, 115n30

Rickover Academy, 141-43

Index

Index

University of Chicago Charter
School, 122-23, 149n8
University of Nebraska, 72
UNO. *See* National Opposition
Union
Urban Institute, 2, 27, 29, 136
Urban Land Institute, 38
USA Patriot Act, 11
Utt, Ronald, 49

Vallas, Paul, 145
Vitale, David, 126
vouchers, 4; criticism of, 29; functions of, 29; housing, 132-33; in
New Orleans, 5, 29-39; promotion of, 34-35

Walton, John, 30, 63n28
war on terrorism, 69
Washington consensus, 8-9, 88
Wells, Amy Stuart, 55
Wells (Ida B.) housing develop-
ment, 121
white supremacy, neoliberalism
and, 47, 67n82
Wood, Elizabeth, 131
Wood, John, 46
workfare, 124
World Bank, 9, 103

Yankee Institute, 32

Zehr, Mary Ann, 100

About the Author

✧

Kenneth Saltman is an associate professor in the Department of Educational Policy Studies and Research at DePaul University in Chicago, where he teaches in the Social and Cultural Foundations of Education graduate program. He is the author of *The Edison Schools* (Routledge, 2005), *Strange Love, or How We Learn to Stop Worrying and Love the Market* (Rowman & Littlefield, 2002), and *Collateral Damage: Corporatizing Public Schools—A Threat to Democracy* (Rowman & Littlefield, 2000) and the editor of *Schooling and the Politics of Disaster* (Routledge, 2007), *The Critical Middle School Reader* (Routledge, 2005), and *Education as Enforcement: The Militarization and Corporatization of Schools* (Routledge, 2003). He is a fellow of the Education Policy Research Unit (EPRU).